The Gen X Series

CYBER OLYMPIAD 2

Useful for Cyber Olympiads Conducted at School, National & International Levels

Authors
Shikha Gupta
Shikha Nautiyal

Peer Reviewer
Manasvi Vohra

Strictly According to the Latest Syllabus of Cyber Olympiad

Published by:

V&S PUBLISHERS

F-2/16, Ansari road, Daryaganj, New Delhi-110002
☎ 23240026, 23240027 • *Fax:* 011-23240028
✉ info@vspublishers.com • 🌐 www.vspublishers.com

Online Brandstore: amazon.in/vspublishers

Regional Office : Hyderabad
5-1-707/1, Brij Bhawan (Beside Central Bank of India Lane)
Bank Street, Koti, Hyderabad - 500 095
☎ 040-24737290
✉ vspublishershyd@gmail.com

Follow us on:   

BUY OUR BOOKS FROM: AMAZON   FLIPKART

© **Copyright:** *V&S* PUBLISHERS
ISBN 978-93-579406-0-3
New Edition

DISCLAIMER

Publisher's Note

General Trade and Mass Appeal books across various genres have helped **V&S Publishers** to gain widespread popularity. In a short span of 10 years, we have successfully published more than 1000 titles across 9 languages in our 50 subject categories. Being into the publishing business for about 40 years, we have always been a dynamic publishing house, with a massive distribution network, across India; including E-commerce platforms.

Understanding the need of inculcating knowledge and developing a spirit of healthy competition amongst students to make them ready for the world outside schools and colleges; we created Olympiad Series under the **GEN X SERIES Imprint** which, owning to its rich content and unique representation became popular amongst students, in no time. The motivation is not to improve marks in terms of numbers, but is to make sure that the students are already prepared to face competitive environment with respect to college admissions and cracking various entrance examinations, while ensuring their conceptual clarity.

Published for classes 1-10 across subjects English, Mathematics, Science, Computers, General Knowledge, the books are unlike any other in the market and are written in a guidebook pattern and exhaustively include examples and Multiple-Choice Questions.

Here, we present the latest Edition of **CYBER OLYMPIAD CLASS 2.**

Unique Features of the book are as follows:

- ☞ Authored by Subject Matter Experts' and Peer reviewed by School Principals and HOD's for the respective subjects
- ☞ Books based on principles of Applied Psychology and Bloom's Taxonomy
- ☞ Suited for Olympiad Examinations held at School level, National level & International Level irrespective of organizing body.
- ☞ The only Olympiad Book in India written in Guidebook Pattern with Concise Theory, images and illustrations.
- ☞ Exhaustively include Examples, MCQs, Subjective Questions, and HOTS with Answer Keys & Solutions.
- ☞ Multiple Model Papers for thorough practice also given inside the book with solutions.
- ☞ OMR sheets appended at the end of the book for simulating exam environment.

Besides, we are also planning to launch an App very soon for the Olympiad preparation which further testifies our constant endeavor to keep up with student demands. We have made sure to closely follow syllabus patterns of not only Olympiad conducting bodies but also education boards & organizations like CBSE and NCERT, to make sure that our books prove useful to students; helping them to boost their academic performance in schools as well.

P.S. While every care has been taken to ensure the correctness of the content, if you come across any error, howsoever minor, do not hesitate to discuss with teachers while pointing that out to us in no uncertain terms.

We wish you All the Best!

DISTINCTIVE

01 LEARNING OBJECTIVES

They list the whole chapter as subtopics, helping the teachers to guide children in a step-by-step manner.

02 DID YOU KNOW

Enhance your knowledge by getting acquainted with some amazing facts across various subjects like science, Mathematics and English.

03 MULTIPLE CHOICE QUESTIONS

MCQs act as an excellent learning aid, helping you to understand and work on your mistakes.

04 THINGS TO REMEMBER

A quick recap of the chapter in a summarized format helps in faster revision along with conceptual clarity.

05 HOTS

The High Order Thinking Questions aim to help the student to solve Application-based questions and gain practical understanding of the subject.

FEATURES

SUBJECTIVE QUESTIONS
Help to place the knowledge gained in orderly fashion by using **"WH"** questions, mostly in the form of bullet points.

06

ACHIEVER'S SECTION
Offers a quick revision of the book along with some new facts for the students to discover.

07

A SET OF OMR SHEETS
To allow the student to practice question in an exam-like format which would help them to get the "feel" of how Olympiad exams take place.

08

MODEL TEST PAPERS
Two model test papers are provided at the end of each book, which help the student to test the knowledge which they have gained after thorough reading of all chapters.

09

ANSWER KEY & SOLUTION
Detailed Answer Key along with explanations aid the pupil to indentify, understand the mistakes they make during the course of Olympiad preparation.

10

COMPLEMENT SCHOOL SYLLABI
The syllabi across all Olympiad examination closely follow the pattern of academic books. Hence, they not only provide a competitive examination experience, but also help to revise topics for school examinations as well, while strengthening conceptual precision.

ENHANCEMENT OF ANALYTICAL & LOGICAL REASONING
Practicing analytical ability questions, not only helps in developing intellectual ability but also plays a vital role in building critical thinking ability which helps an individual to think about a question or a crisis like situation in day to day life; from all aspects and directions.

Note to Parents

Dear Parents,

Olympiad examinations come with a plethora of advantages. First and foremost among such advantages is the application of knowledge studied, in the form of multiple-choice questions. It helps the child not only to step away from rote learning, but also helps them to exhibit their competencies across various subjects.

In addition to this, Olympiads help the student to understand the importance of revision and practice, and to imbibe upon these practices; which also prove useful in academic performance of the child.

The Olympiads are conducted across multiple subjects, and help the child to recognize their field of interest, thereby encouraging the students to make a career in the field where they can excel the most.

However, cognitive development of a child is not just limited to the four walls of classroom. Following steps can be encouraged by you, to ensure their ward is able to grasp various concepts with ease or lesser difficulty:

☞ **Eat a balanced diet:** Ensure intake of vitamins and minerals to keep you active. Include fruits and super foods like millet in your diet to ensure healthy functioning of organs. Huge intake of junk food should be avoided.

☞ **Indulge in outdoor activities:** Outdoor games break the monotony of life. Play your heart out in greenery to keep yourself alert, active and fit.

☞ **Sleep well:** A sound sleep of 7-8 hours refreshes the brain and makes it ready to understand new topics with more clarity. A sleep derived person faces difficulty in doing even the simplest tasks of day to day life.

☞ **Reduce your Screen time:** More screen time leads to not only weakening of eyesight but decreases concentration span. Regulated Screen time should be encouraged

☞ **Do not hesitate to raise a hand:** Having a doubt in class? Do not hesitate to ask your parents or teachers. This ensures more Conceptual Clarity and hence leads to Application based understanding of various subjects and topics.

☞ **Teach and Learn:** No need to do rote-learning. Once you understand a topic teach or explain it to your friends, siblings and parents. It brings clarity and ensures the child does his revision this way.

☞ **Keep smiling:** A positive attitude promotes a growth mindset and encourages the child to be more inquisitive and try to learn something new, everyday!

HAPPY LEARNING!

Contents

SECTION 1: COMPUTERS AND IT

1.	Introduction to Computer	9
2.	Fundamentals of Computer	16
3.	Parts of a Computer	23
4.	Uses of Computer	32
5.	Learning to Use Keyboard	40
6.	Learning to Use Mouse	47
7.	Introduction to MS Paint	53
8.	Latest Developments in IT	61

SECTION 2: LOGICAL REASONING

1.	Patterns	69
2.	Odd One Out	73
3.	Series Completion	76
4.	Analogy	79
5.	Coding and Decoding	82
6.	Ranking Test	85
7.	Embedded Figures	89
8.	Grouping of Figures	93
9.	Measuring Units	98
10.	Geometrical Shapes	103

SECTION 3: ACHIEVER'S SECTION

Achiever's Section	110
Model Test Paper-1	115
Model Test Paper-2	120
ANSWER KEYS (Access Content online on Dropbox)	125
APPENDIX	130

SECTION 1
COMPUTERS AND IT

Introduction to Computer 1

CHAPTER SUMMARY

We often visit shopping malls, railway stations, airports and hospitals. At these places, we see various screens flashing text and numbers. These screens are actually computer-operated screens. The computer is an amazing machine that helps us perform several tasks with great ease.

What is a computer?

Computer is an electronic machine just like mobiles, television and tablets that takes instructions from users and performs a task. But a computer is different from these electronic devices. Let us discuss what makes a computer a unique electronic device.

1. A computer helps us to carry out difficult calculations in a fraction of second.

2. A computer is a source of entertainment as we can play games on it; watch movies and listen to music.

3. We can be creative with computers. Just as we draw on a paper, we can make drawings on a computer, too.

4. Computer helps us to explore information about the world and helps us to communicate with our friends who are at distant places.

Overall, a computer is a wholesome electronic machine that helps us read, write, draw, see, learn and enjoy.

1 out of 8 people in the United States met online.

Types of Computer

There are several types of computers. Computer shape and size is evolving day by day. Earlier, computers used to be very big in size but slowly their size reduced and the functioning improved. Some of the common types of computers are:

Supercomputer

This is one of the fastest and the biggest computer in terms of memory and speed. A Supercomputer is mainly used for weather forecasting, aircraft designing, etc.

Examples of supercomputers are CRAY and PARAM.

Mainframe Computer

This computer is smaller than the supercomputer but they are a group of computers connected to one main computer.

Personal Computer (PC) or Desktop

It is a small computer that is seen generally in offices and homes. It is made for individual use.

Laptop

It is a portable small-sized computer, which is very handy and can be carried anywhere. It is very similar to a desktop in its functions.

Palmtop

It is a very small hand-held computer that stores little amount of information and having limited functionality than the other computer.

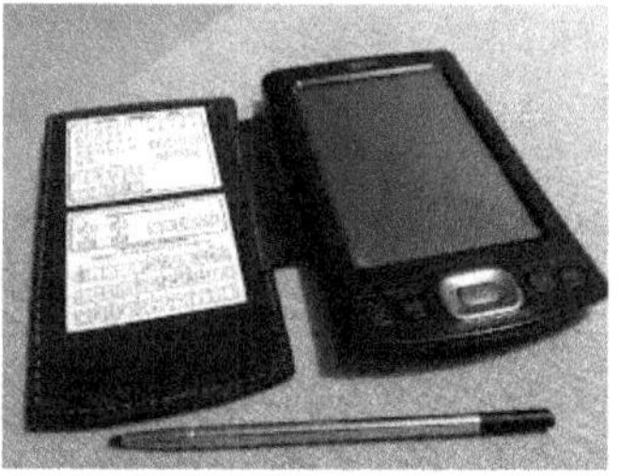

Tablet

It is a thin and touch screen-operated computer. You can get connected with the entire world using a tablet.

Touch screen: It is a device that displays pictures and text and correspondingly responses to human touch. The screen of the device is highly responsive to the finger touch.

Computer Versus Man

Computer is a man-made machine. Some of the basic features of a computer that make it different from a human being are:

Speed

A computer works at a very high speed; it can carry out complex calculations in a very short time.

Tiredness

Since computer is a machine, it never gets tired, it can work non-stop for several hours. There are some computers that work round the clock whereas a human being gets tired after working for a long period.

Mistakes

Computer performs the tasks according to the instructions given by its user. A computer never makes mistakes.

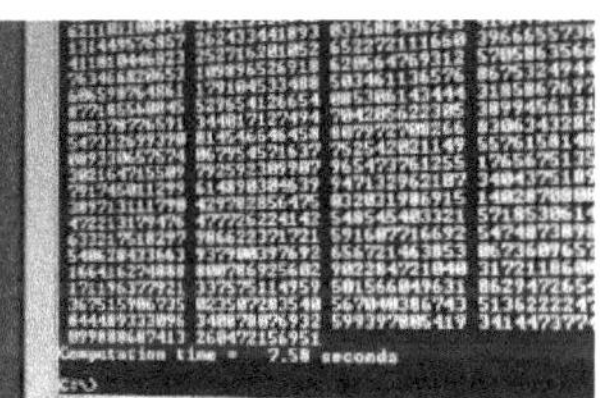

Memory

Computer has a good memory system; it stores the information and remembers it forever. A human being can forget but a computer can never forget any information.

But yes, there are certain points where a human being is far superior to a computer. When we talk about who is superior, it is always a human being who is superior as a computer works on the commands given to it whereas human beings take decisions on their own.

A computer is dependent on an electrical source for its functioning. If there is no electric supply, a computer cannot function.

Abbreviations:
CPU : Central Processing Unit
ALU : Arithmetic Logical Unit
MU : Memory Unit
VDU : Visual Display Unit
KB : Kilobyte
MB : Mega Byte
GB : Giga Byte

- Computer is an electronic machine just like mobiles, television and tablets that takes instructions from users and performs a task.
- This is one of the fastest and the biggest computer in terms of memory and speed.
- Since computer is a machine, it never gets tired.
- A computer never makes mistakes.

MULTIPLE CHOICE QUESTIONS

1. Which is the most powerful in terms of memory?
   (a) Desktop
   (b) Palmtop
   (c) Tablet
   (d) Mainframe computer

2. Which computer has the smallest screen?

   (a)  Tablet
   (b)  Desktop
   (c)  Laptop
   (d)  Mainframe computer

3. Which task cannot be performed by a computer?
   (a) Drawing images
   (b) Writing letters
   (c) Illuminating a room
   (d) Calculating sums

4. Find the odd one out.

   (a)  Palmtop
   (b) 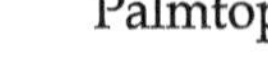 Laptop
   (c)  Calculator
   (d) 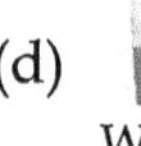 Washing Machine

5. A computer cannot
   (a) Work tirelessly
   (b) Remember everything
   (c) Run fast
   (d) Calculate fast

6. Unjumble the word and find out which is not a type of computer.
   (a) PLAOTP
   (b) DSPTKEO
   (c) TLVISOEEIN
   (d) BTTLEA

7. This is not an electronic machine.

   (a)  Bicycle
   (b)  Microwave
   (c)  Mobile phone
   (d) Laptop

8. This abbreviation does not relate to computers.
   (a) VDU
   (b) ALU
   (c) BSc
   (d) Kb

9. Tick the place where we do not see a computer.
   (a) Superstore
   (b) Airport
   (c) Temple
   (d) Drawing room

10. This feature is uncommon between a man and a computer.
    (a) Memory
    (b) Calculation
    (c) Voice
    (d) Emotions

11. Which computer type is best suited for an airport?

    (a)  Laptop
    (b)  Mainframe computer
    (c) 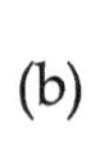 Desktop
    (d)  Supercomputer

12. Ravi is a class 2 student. Which type of computer should he use to learn the basic functioning of a computer?
    (a) Supercomputer
    (b) Laptop
    (c) Desktop
    (d) Tablet

13. Which type of computer has a touch screen?
    (a) Palmtop   (b) Tablet
    (c) Laptop   (d) All of them
14. We find several punching keys on the
    (a) Washing machine
    (b) Calculator
    (c) Desktop
    (d) (b) and (c) both
15. A computer cannot search
    (a) Lost file
    (b) Lost image
    (c) Lost key
    (d) Lost document
16. While working on a computer, we should not
    (a) work in bright light
    (b) keep the computer clean
    (c) sit straight
    (d) bend forward towards the screen
17. Which is the best statement to define a computer?
    (a) A computer is a man-made electronic device.
    (b) A computer is a man-made electronic device that can store a lot of data.
    (c) A computer is an electronic device.
    (d) A computer is a smart device.
18. This cannot be a computer game.
    (a) Car race
    (b) Creative art
    (c) Bike race
    (d) Hide-N-Seek
19. This computer has several wires.
    (a) Laptop
    (b) Mainframe computer
    (c) Desktop
    (d) Tablet
20. This term is not related to computers.
    (a) Speed   (b) Memory
    (c) Fatigue   (d) File

1. Which option will process this information faster?

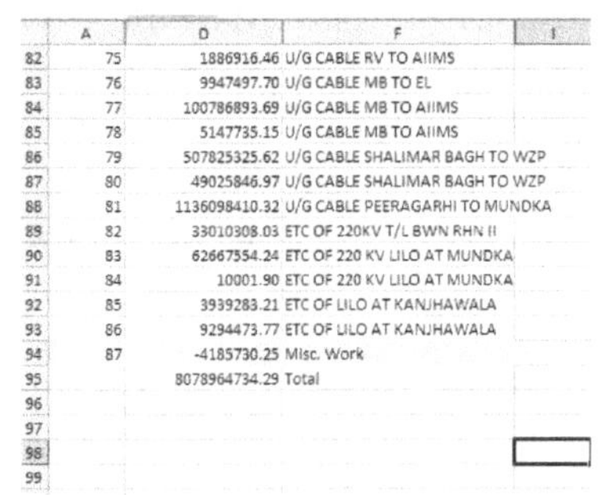

(a)

(b)

Calculator   Computer

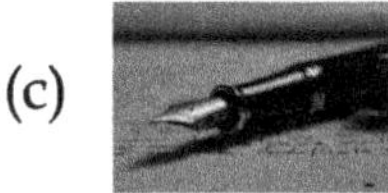
(c)

(d)

Paper pen   Typewriter

2. Identify the devices marked as X and Y with the help of given information.

Device X	Device Y
It is not portable.	It comes with a touchpad.

(a) Device X -    Device Y -

(b) Device X -   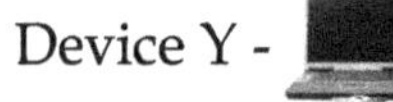 Device Y -

(c) Device X -    Device Y - 

(d) Device X -    Device Y -

3. Select the hand-held device that can be connected with the desktop computer using a wire (known as data cable).

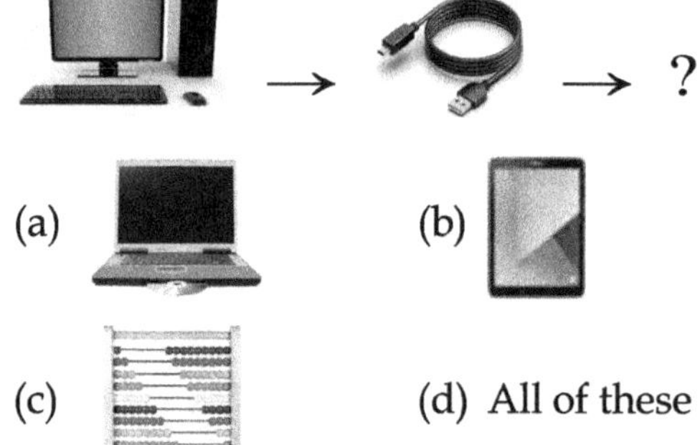

(a)   (b)

(c)   (d) All of these

4. To which location does a deleted file is stored when we DELETE a file?

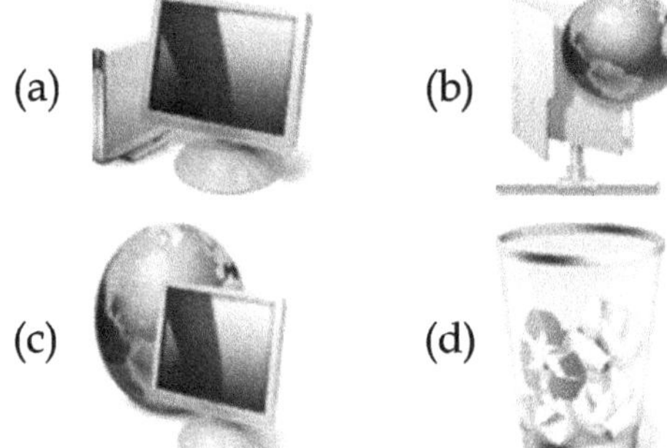

(a)   (b)

(c)   (d)

5. Speed of Laser Printer is measured in which unit?

(a) LPM   (b) DPS
(c) DPI   (d) PPM

1. **What is a computer? Explain in brief.**

Ans.

A computer is a complex machine that makes our lives easier by making difficult tasks simple for us. It also lets us play games, watch movies, and listen to music, among a whole lot of other things. It is difficult to imagine a life without computers because they are so useful to humans.

2. **Name the three types of computers.**

Ans.

Desktop computer, Laptop computer, Tablet Computer

   i. Desktop computer – A desktop computer is a big computer and they require electricity to work. Desktop computers are generally fixed in one place because they have a lot of wires.

   ii. Laptop computer – A laptop computer is a small and more flexible computer than a desktop computer. A laptop computer runs on a battery that can be charged with a charger.

   iii. Tablet Computer – A tablet computer is the smallest form of a computer machine and it does not have an external keyboard.

3. **Fill in the blanks with right option:**

   (a) A ——————— is a machine (computer, book)

   (b) A computer never gets ——————— (tired, lazy)

   (c) A computer makes our work very ——————— (easy, difficult)

   (d) A computer works very ——————— (fast, slow)

Ans.

   (a) A computer is a machine.

   (b) A computer never gets tired.

   (c) A computer makes our work very easy.

   (d) A computer works very fast.

4. **Put a Tick (✓) mark and Wrong (✗) mark for the following sentences**

   (a) Computer works on electricity.

   (b) Computer makes our work very difficult.

   (c) Computer cannot remember many things.

   (d) Computer is used for solving big mathematical sums.

Ans.

   (a) Computer works on electricity. (✓)

   (b) Computer makes our work very difficult. (✗)

   (c) Computer cannot remember many things. (✗)

   (d) Computer is used for solving big mathematical sums. (✓)

Fundamentals of Computer

2

Learning Objectives : In this chapter, students will learn about:
- ✓ Starting a Computer
- ✓ Shutting Down a Desktop
- ✓ IPO Cycle
- ✓ General Information on Computer

CHAPTER SUMMARY

A desktop is also known as a personal computer. It is commonly found at home or in the computer lab at school. The first step towards using a desktop is to learn how to start it and how to shut it down. A computer runs on electrical supply. It is recommended to start a computer in the presence of an elder so that we are guided well.

Starting a Computer

Every desktop has five basic parts: UPS, CPU, monitor, keyboard and mouse. All these parts are connected with each other through wires.

1. The first step is to 'switch ON' the power supply switch. It is recommended that this step be carried out by your elders. Also keep in mind to never switch ON a power switch with wet hands as you might get an electrical shock.

2. After switching on the power switch, next comes the UPS. There is a switch on the UPS which has to be pushed 'ON'.

> **What does it mean?**
> UPS means Uninterrupted Power Supply unit which provides power to the desktop in the absence of electricity.

3. Then we will switch ON the CPU, the central processing unit of the computer, which monitors the functioning of all the other parts of the computer.

4. The monitor, resembling a TV screen is also switched ON after switching ON the CPU.

The screen of the monitor resembles the image given below.

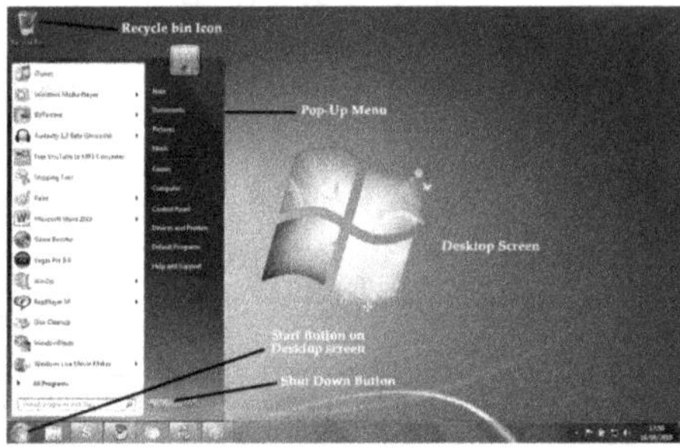

A computer takes some time to start. This start-up time is known as **Booting**. While booting, a computer prepares everything in its memory for our usage. This also means that a CPU prepares itself for functioning. This is also called Warm-Booting.

> The other options that we come across while shutting down a computer are:
> Hibernate: A process to standby the computer, that is stopping its functioning temporarily to save power, especially when we are not going to use the computer for a few hours.
> Cold Booting: The pressing of the power button is called Cold Booting, in technical terms.

Shutting Down a Desktop

The shutting down of a desktop starts in the reverse manner.

1. The **'Start button'** indicated on the monitor screen, is **'double-clicked'** through a mouse pointer. A dialogue box opens. The **'Shut down'** option is clicked with the mouse pointer and the windows screen starts shutting down.

   This means the CPU is preparing itself to stop all its functions.

2. The monitor switch is 'switched OFF' once the screen is black.

   The monitor's power button is known as a Toggle Button. This Toggle Button should be switched OFF while closing the computer.

3. After this the CPU switch is 'switched OFF', followed by 'switching OFF' of the UPS.

4. Finally, the main power switch is 'switched OFF'.

IPO Cycle

After starting a computer, a computer follows a specific route to function. This specific route is called the IPO cycle. **IPO** means: **Input-Process-Output**.

Input means providing information or instructions to the computer.

Process means processing or calculating the information.

Output means giving results.

This can be depicted easily with the following diagram:

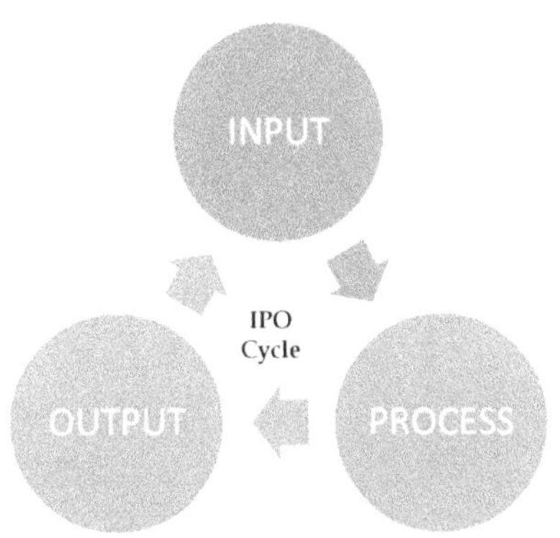

In case of a desktop: The data or information is fed into the computer through a keyboard, which is then processed in the CPU and the result or output is shown on the monitor.

General Information on Computer

While working on a computer, we should be familiar with certain general information related to it. This information is summarised below:

- Pressing CTRL+ALT+DEL key simultaneously results in opening of the following screen:

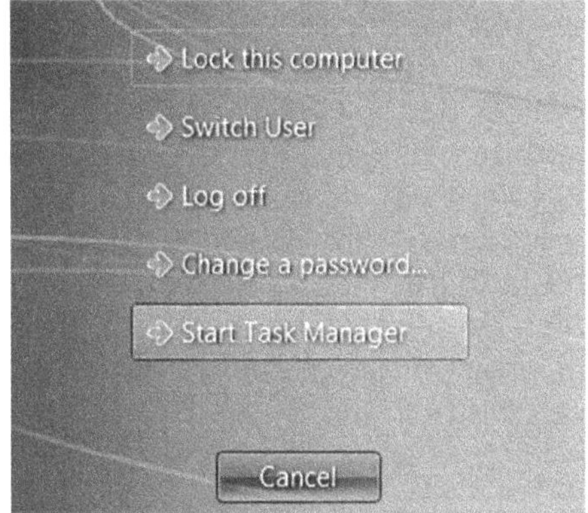

  This function helps us to Lock this computer, Switch user, Log off, Change password, or Start task manager.

- A desktop screen has the following components displayed on it: icons (small boxes which could be software, a recycle bin, files and folders); a taskbar (placed at the bottom of the screen. At the left end of the Taskbar, a 'Start button' is located that gives us access to all the programs available on the computer); a system tray (displays time) and a wallpaper (a picture or base screen on which icons and taskbar is located).

- After booting, sometimes a computer asks for login and password, which means, the computer wants to confirm about you. Login ID and password increase the security of the computer and it cannot be used by a stranger.

- The keyboard is the input device. The monitor is the output device. The display clarity of a monitor is defined by pixels. The more the pixels the clearer the image.

- The data that is fed into the CPU follows a binary system that is a code language possessing only two numbers: 0 and 1.
- The CPU which is the main processing centre of the information has three main parts: Arithmetic Logical Unit (ALU), Control Unit (CU) and Memory Unit (MU).
- The CPU is also called the microprocessor because the CPU is placed on a small chip (1 inch square in dimension). This chip is made up of silicon.
- The unit of the memory of the CPU is measured in bytes. The more the bytes, the more data a CPU can store.
- Computer is an advanced calculating device that carries out complex calculations. The basic and the first calculating device was invented in China which is called **Abacus**. The Abacus is still used in basic levels of education to teach mathematics.

Only about 10% of the world's currency is physical money, the rest only exists on computers.

- The first computer was invented by Charles Babbage. He is known as the **'father of computer'**.
- The unit to measure the speed of the computer, which means the speed at which the data will be processed in the computer CPU, is Hertz and is denoted by Hz.

➤ A computer takes some time to start up. This start-up time is known as Booting. While booting, a computer prepares everything in its memory for our usage. This also means that a CPU prepares itself for functioning. This is also called Warm-Booting.

➤ After starting a computer, a computer follows a specific route to function. This specific route is called the IPO cycle. IPO means: Input-Process-Output.

1. Find the odd one out.
   (a) Power   (b) Toggle
   (c) Switch   (d) Goggle

2. UPS, CPU, monitor, keyboard and all other computer devices are connected with
   (a) Power button   (b) Wires
   (c) Chips   (d) Magnets

3. The first calculating device was
   (a) Calculator   (b) Typewriter
   (c) Desktop   (d) Abacus

4. Icons are present on the
   (a) Desktop main screen
   (b) Taskbar
   (c) System tray
   (d) All of them

5. The following icon is of:

   (a) System tray   (b) Folder
   (c) File   (d) Software

6. Look at the image below and write what command will lead you to this:

   (a) Ctrl+ALT+Del
   (b) Start button ☐ Shut down
   (c) Start button ☐ Hibernate
   (d) CTRL+Del

7. What does this icon mean on the desktop?

   (a) An icon
   (b) A software
   (c) A hardware
   (d) A mouse pointer

8. This is the unit for memory.
   (a) Byte   (b) Hertz
   (c) Metre   (d) Kilogram

9. Pixel is related to which part of the computer?
   (a) Keyboard   (b) CPU
   (c) Monitor   (d) UPS

10. UPS stands for
    (a) Uninterrupted power supply
    (b) Unhindered power supply
    (c) Unwanted power supply
    (d) Unique power supply

11. Observe the sequence below. Which option follows the IPO cycle?

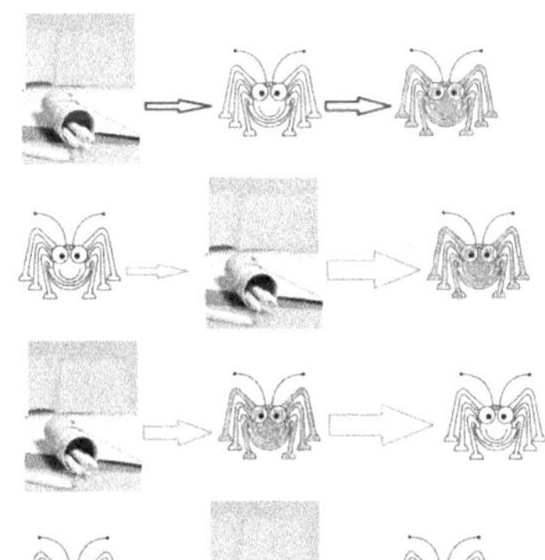

(a) 

(b) 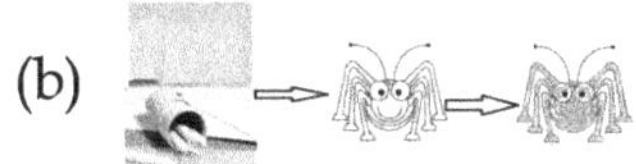

(c) 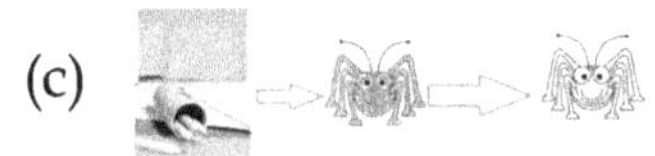

(d) 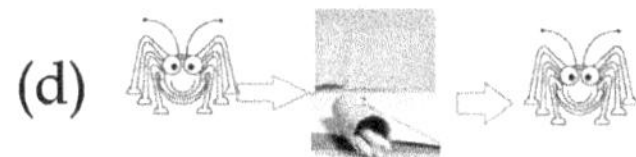

12. Which option is correctly matched?
    (a) Monitor-Input; Printer-Output; CPU-Process
    (b) Keyboard-Input; CPU-process; Monitor-Output
    (c) Mouse-Input; CPU-Process; Keyboard-Output
    (d) Mouse-Input; CPU-Process and Output

13. In the image given below, what are X, Y and Z?

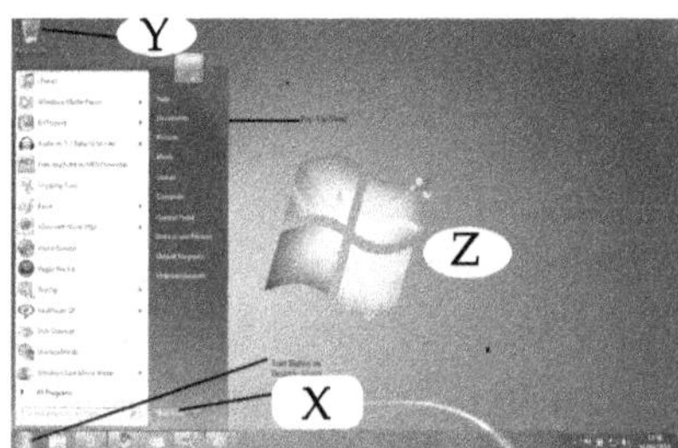

	X	Y	Z
(a)	Switch off	Boot button	Screensaver button
(b)	Start Button	Icon	Wallpaper
(c)	Shut Down Button	Icon	Desktop Screen
(d)	Icon	Boot Button	Wallpaper

14. The time taken by a CPU to ready itself for functioning is called
    (a) Cold Boot
    (b) Warm Boot
    (c) Hibernate
    (d) Start up

15. 'Switching ON' of the power switch is called
    (a) Start Up   (b) Switch User
    (c) Cold Boot   (d) Warm Boot

16. The area of desktop that displays the time
    (a) Taskbar
    (b) System Tray
    (c) Icon
    (d) Pop-up Menu

17. Name the language understood by a computer.
    (a) Binary digits: Machine language
    (b) Alphabets
    (c) Numeric
    (d) Tertiary digits: Machine language

18. Which can be a code related to computer language?
    (a) A1001A   (b) 101010
    (c) 1016101017   (d) FGFTDRRFV

19. What is ALU and what is its location?

		I	II
(a)	Arithmetic Logical Unit		Monitor
(b)	Arithmetic Logic Unit		CPU
(c)	Arithmetic Language		CPU
(d)	Arithmetic Logic Unit		Keyboard

20. This cannot be an input device.

(a) 
Keyboard

(b) 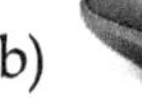 
Mouse

(c)  
Laptop Touchpad

(d) 
Printer

1. Ravi's father suffered from severe backache, his doctor recommended him not to use the computer, what could be the possible reason?

   I. He worked for long hours on the computer.

   II. He did not sit properly while working on the computer.

   III. He played games on computers.

   (a) I and II   (b) I and III

   (c) I   (d) II

2. Mr A and Mr B are neighbours. They both work on computers the whole day. They use the same electrical gadgets. But Mr. A's computer battery drains faster than Mr. B's. Why?

   I. Electric cuts are more in Mr. B's house.

   II. Mr. A does not 'hibernate' the computer when not in use.

   III. Mr B 'hibernates' the computer when not in use.

   IV. Mr. A's computer battery may be old.

   (a) I, II and III   (b) I and III

   (c) II, III and IV   (d) III and IV

3. A group of 5 students were trying some codes. Identify which student can directly relate his/her code to computer language.

Student name	Code
Chang	ag6t21bi9hydxnb
John	FGTUYFFTUYIK
Lily	10101011111
Tina	0001100000
Sam	O)O)OHUGF^CD$%

   (a) Tina and Sam

   (b) John and Lily

   (c) Lily and Sam

   (d) Lily and Tina

4. Which of the following shows the CORRECT order of IPO cycle?

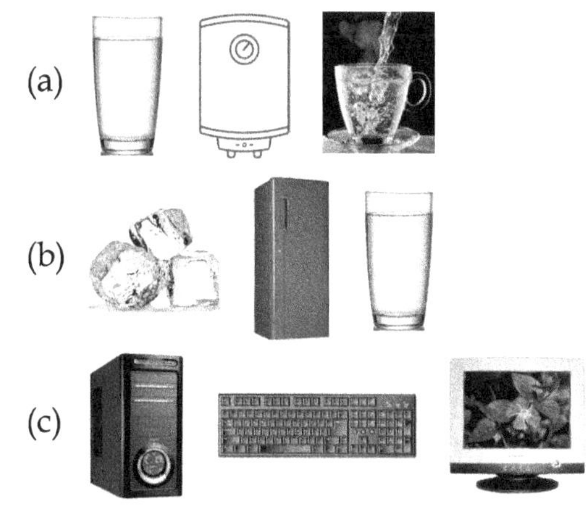

   (d) All of these

5. In the given image, box marked as 'X' requires the secret series of characters in order to have access to the computer. This secret series of characters is known as ______.

   (a) Password   (b) Wallpaper

   (c) Context   (d) Tools

1. What are the steps involved in switching of a computer?

Ans.

The following is the correct procedure to switch ON the computer:

(a) Switch ON the main power switch.

(b) Press the ON button on the UPS of the computer.

(c) Press the ON button on the CPU of the computer.

(d) Switch ON the Monitor.

(e) After some time, a screen will appear on the monitor. This screen is called the desktop.

(f) Desktop is the first screen that you see on the computer when Windows has loaded.

2. What steps are followed to shut down a computer?

Ans.

To shut down the computer the following steps should be followed:

(a) Click Start button.

(b) When the start menu appears, click shut down. When the shut down box appears, click OK.

(c) Switch OFF the Monitor.

(d) Switch OFF the CPU of the computer.

(e) Switch OFF the main power button.

3. What is a Super Computer?

Ans.

Supercomputer is the fastest and the most powerful computer. It is the biggest in size and more expensive in price than any other computer. It is used to perform complex task. It has an exceptionally large storage capacity. It can process trillions of instructions in one second. Example: Roadrunner, Deep blue etc.

4. What is cache memory?

Ans.

Cache is high-speed memory that holds the most recent data and instructions that have been loaded by the CPU. It is designed to speed up the transfer of data and instructions. Cache is found directly on the CPU or between the CPU and RAM. It is faster than RAM

5. What do you mean by resolution of monitor?

Ans.

Resolution is an important characteristic of any display device. The number of pixels displayed on screen is called screen resolution. Resolution decides the amount of information that can be displayed at one time.

Parts of a Computer

Learning Objectives : In this chapter, students will learn about:
- ✓ Input Devices
- ✓ Processing Device
- ✓ Storage Devices
- ✓ Output Devices

CHAPTER SUMMARY

A computer is a machine that has several parts. These parts are connected with each other through wires. The parts are divided into three sections as per their functions, that is: Input-Process-Output.

Input Devices

The devices that put in information into the computer are called Input devices. They are: keyboard, mouse, scanner and microphone. The keyboard and the mouse are standard devices of the computer. The scanner and the microphone are accessory devices of the computer.

Keyboard

It is an essential input device of the computer. The keyboard resembles a typewriter.

Typewriter

Keyboard

The basic function of a keyboard is to feed information into a computer by typing letters, numbers and symbols.

> Alphabet keys: A, B, C, D...
> Number keys: 1, 2, 3, 4 ...
> Symbol keys: !, @, $, % ...

Along with the alphabet, number and symbol keys, the keyboard has several other keys to carry out special functions.

Mouse

It is another input device that resembles the shape of a mouse. It is connected with a cable to the CPU of the computer. The mouse body and the cable give an appearance of a tailed mouse. When we move a mouse, its movement is indicated by an arrow or a pointer on the monitor screen. This movement of mouse pointer on the monitor screen helps us to carry out several functions such as opening a file, a folder or even playing a game.

Scanner

A scanner is a unique input device which acts as a camera. For example, if we place a photograph on the scanner, the photograph gets captured and is flashed on the monitor screen.

Microphone

Microphone is a voice-based device that resembles a mic. It is a device that records voice, sound and music in the computer. It is found in offices and also at home.

Joystick

It is a gaming device that helps us to play games on the computer. It has a movable handle with buttons on it that help us to move our gaming characters swiftly on the monitor screen.

Web camera

It is a camera that is connected with the computer. It captures our images and sends it to our friends through the internet.

Trackball

It is an input device mostly used in laptops. It also acts as a mouse but resembles a ball in shape.

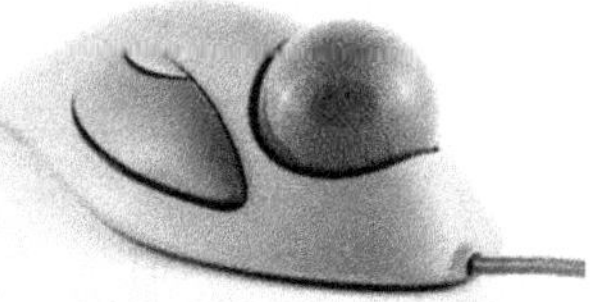

Power Supply Device: UPS

It is an important device required in a desktop as desktop does not have a built in battery like a laptop.

Processing Device

Processing device is a device that works on the information fed into it through the input devices. CPU (Central Processing Unit) is the main processing centre of the computer.

For example, if we want to carry out addition of numbers: 1, 2 and 3.

The addition of these numbers is done by the CPU.

$1 + 2 + 3 = 6$.

The result '6' is then displayed on the monitor.

The main parts of a CPU are

(a) ALU: Arithmetic Logic Unit - Carries out calculations.

(b) CU: Control Unit - Controls functioning of CPU.

(c) Stores information.

Storage Devices

The information in the CPU is stored in storage devices. The inbuilt storage device of the CPU is the hard drive which stores a lot of information. The unit of information is bytes, megabytes, and gigabytes. A hard drive cannot be removed easily from the CPU.

The first hard drive could only hold 5MB of data.

The other storage devices are: **CD**, **DVD** and **Blu-ray**. These are the secondary storage devices.

CD:  DVD:

The major difference between a CD and the DVD is the amount of information one can store. A CD has less storage space than a DVD.

Blu ray: 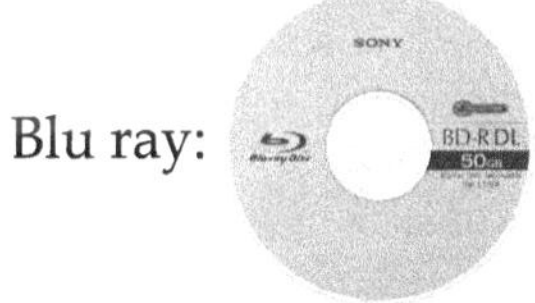

A Blu-ray has the highest storage capacity.

One of the obsolete storage devices is the **Floppy disc**. It stored very less information and is less durable compared to the modern storage devices.

Output Devices

These devices display the work done by the CPU, Hence they are also called the display units.

Monitor

A monitor resembles a television as it has a screen that displays pictures, text, movies, etc. It is also called the Visual Display Unit (VDU).

The modern monitors are flat screened just like LCD (Liquid Crystal Display) or LED (Light Emitting Diode) TVs.

Modern technology has modified the monitor screens. These screens now act as an input as well as output device as they have a touch-sensitive screen which can take in commands through touch.

Speaker

They are sound-producing devices through which we listen to music and hear different sounds, such as dialogues in a movie. Some computer monitors have built-in speakers.

Printer

It is an output device which produces exactly what is displayed on the computer screen. It prints the displayed image or document on paper.

- ➡ The devices that put in information into the computer are called Input devices.
- ➡ When we move a mouse, its movement is indicated by an arrow or a pointer on the monitor screen.
- ➡ A scanner is a unique input device which acts as a camera.
- ➡ Processing device is a device that works on the information fed into it through the input devices. CPU (Central Processing Unit) is the main processing centre of the computer.
- ➡ Speakers are sound-producing devices through which we listen to music and hear different sounds, such as dialogues in a movie.
- ➡ Printer is an output device which produces exactly what is displayed on the computer screen.

1. Look at the desktop image below and find out which part is labelled incorrectly.

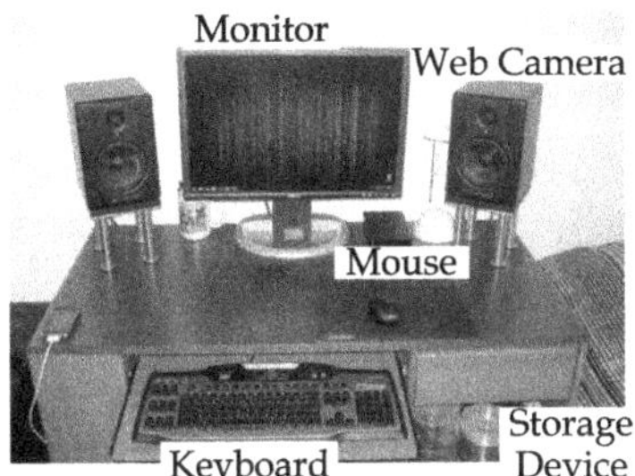

(a) Monitor
(b) Keyboard
(c) Speakers
(d) Mouse

2. This is not an input device.

(a) 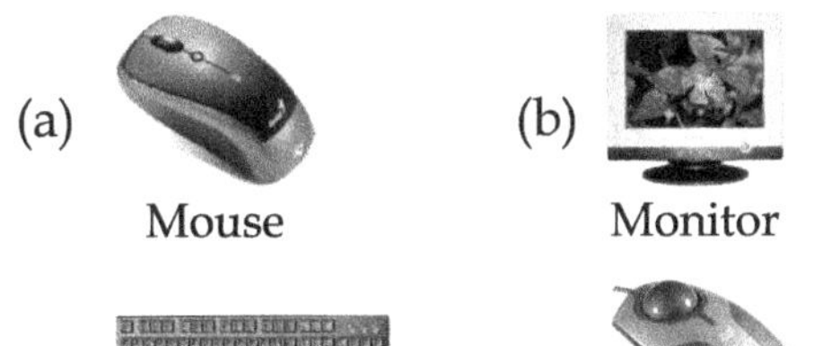
Mouse

(b) Monitor

(c) 
Keyboard

(d) 
Trackball

3. This is an input device.

(a) Elephant
(b) Snake
(c) Cat
(d) Mouse

4. This produces musical sound.

(a) Web camera
(b) Printer
(c) Scanner
(d) Speaker

5. This is not an essential part of a desktop.

(a) 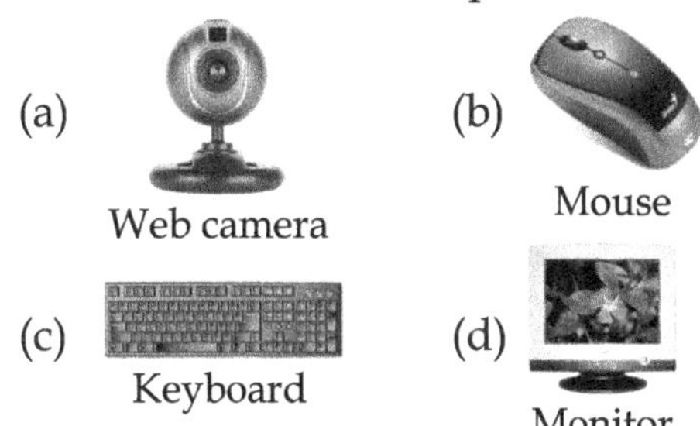
Web camera

(b) Mouse

(c) Keyboard

(d) Monitor

6. Observe the image below. What could it be?

(a) An input device
(b) An output device
(c) A storage device
(d) None of these

7. While playing a game, we use this the most.

(a) 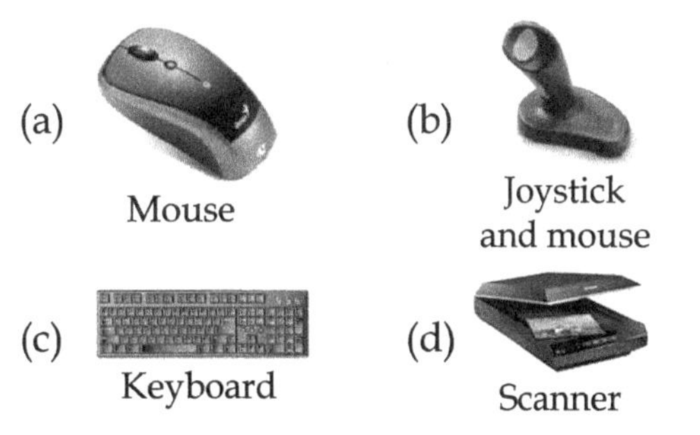
Mouse

(b) Joystick and mouse

(c) Keyboard

(d) Scanner

8. This is not a storage device.

(a) 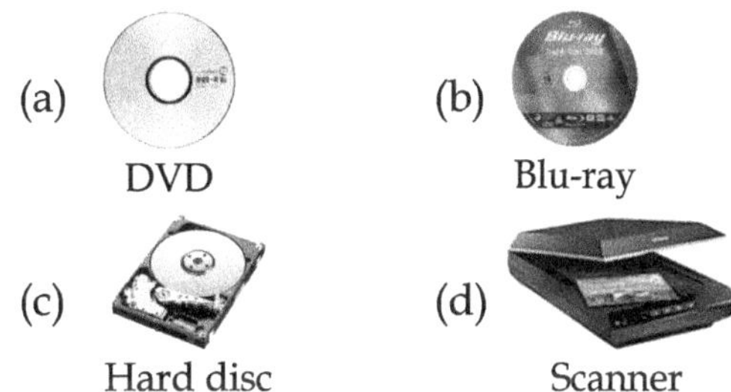
DVD

(b) Blu-ray

(c) Hard disc

(d) Scanner

9. We find !, @, %, ^ type of symbols on the

(a) 
Web camera

(b) 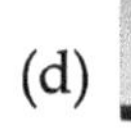
Mouse

(c) 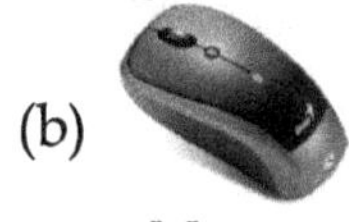
Keyboard

(d) 
Monitor

10. This is the brain of the computer.

(a) 
CPU

(b) 
Mouse

(c) 
Keyboard

(d) 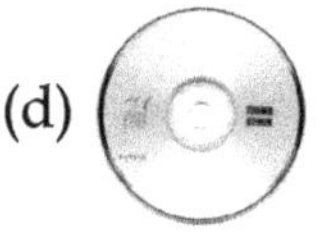
Monitor

11. Match the following

I		II	
(a)	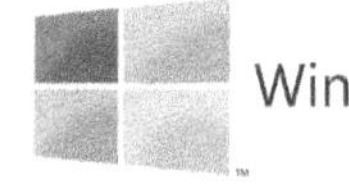	(i)	CD
(b)		(ii)	Mouse
(c)		(iii)	Scanner
(d)		(iv)	Hard disc

(a) a-i, b-ii, c-iii, d-iv
(b) a-ii, b-iii, c-iv, d-i
(c) a-iii, b-i, c-ii, d-iv
(d) a-iv, b-iii, c-ii, d-i

12. Observe the image below. What is it?

Windows®8

(a) Keyboard symbol
(b) Mouse pointer
(c) Desktop screen image
(d) Windows logo

13. It is a circular device which is not attached to the computer with a wire.
(a) Mouse   (b) Track ball
(c) DVD   (d) Web camera

14. This does not belong to the CPU.
(a) ALU   (b) CD
(c) CU   (d) Hard Disc

15. Meena wants to submit a project that she did on her computer, which device will she use?
(a) Scanner   (b) Monitor
(c) Printer   (d) Speaker

16. What is a scanner?
(a) A scanner is a device that transfers the picture kept on its surface to the computer.
(b) A scanner is a device that creates images.
(c) A scanner is a device that helps us to take printouts.
(d) A scanner is a sound-producing device.

17. We store a large amount of data in:

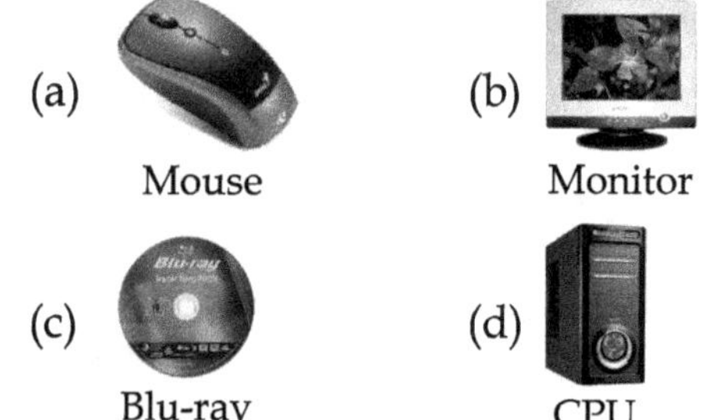

(a) Mouse   (b) Monitor

(c) Blu-ray   (d) CPU

18. To watch a movie, which parts of a computer will you use?
(a) Monitor, Speaker, CPU
(b) Monitor
(c) Printer
(d) CPU

19. I am a unique device. I help you to communicate with others through a computer.

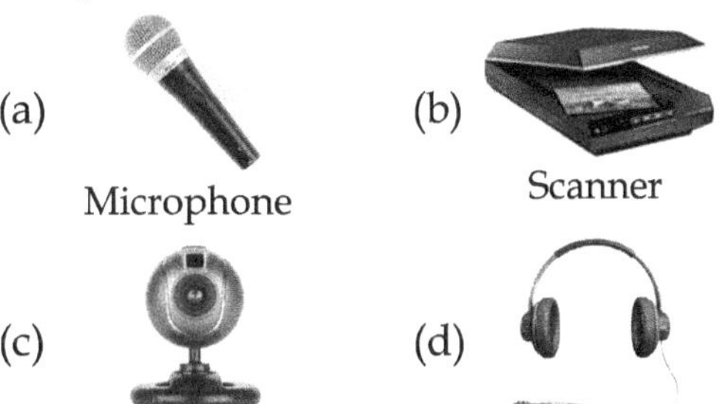

(a) Microphone

(b) Scanner

(c) Web camera

(d) Headphones

20. Which device can store the highest amount of information?
(a) CPU
(b) DVD
(c) CD
(d) Blu-ray

1. There was a grand fun fair going on in a city. A child got lost. The fun fair had computerised cameras installed all over. Which device will the security personnel use to search that child's parents?

(a)  (b)

(c)  (d)

2. With which computer parts does the following image correlate?

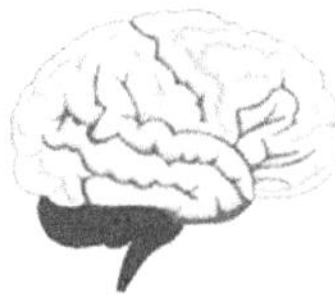

I.   Mouse
II. CD
III. Blu-Ray
IV. CPU
(a) IV
(b) I and II
(c) I
(d) III and IV

3. Which of the following is NOT a part of computer?

(a) 

(b) 

(c) 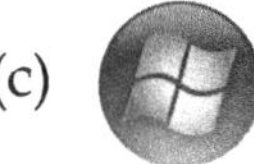

(d)

4. Which of the following states the CORRECT difference between the given two devices?

(a)		
	It is a pointing device.	It is not a pointing device.
(b)		
	It can be connected to the computer.	It cannot be connected to the computer.
(c)		
	It is used to give input to the computer.	It is used to display output to the computer.
(d)		

It can be used to draw pictures on screen.	It cannot be used to draw pictures on screen.

5. Identify the external power supply unit given below that is used to plug the computer into a standard electrical outlet.

(a) Monitor   (b) USB Cable
(c) AC adapter   (d) Keyboard

1. Fill in the blanks by selecting the correct word from the bracket:

   (a) The _______ is kept just next to the monitor and different computer parts are connected to it.
   (CPU, Mouse)

   (b) The _______ Is the part of computer whose shape is just like a rectangle box. (Keyboard, CPU)

   (c) The _______ unit of the CPU is responsible to complete the work in relation to mathematical calculation.
   (ALU, CU)

   (d) CPU stands for _______
   (Central Processing Unit, Centre Processor in Unit)

   (e) The small button on the CPU box is known as _______
   (Reset button, Power button)

Ans.

   (a) The **CPU** is kept just next to the monitor and different computer parts are connected to it.

   (b) The **CPU** is the part of computer whose shape is just like a rectangle box.

   (c) The **ALU** unit of the CPU is responsible to complete the work in relation to mathematical calculation.

   (d) CPU stands for **Central Processing Unit**

   (e) The small button on the CPU box is known as **Reset button**

2. What work do the CPU do out of the following?

Performs Actions	Sleep, Eat and Drink
Play Games	Performs Mathematical Calculations
Run Programs	Watch a Movie
Never works	Saves Information

Ans.

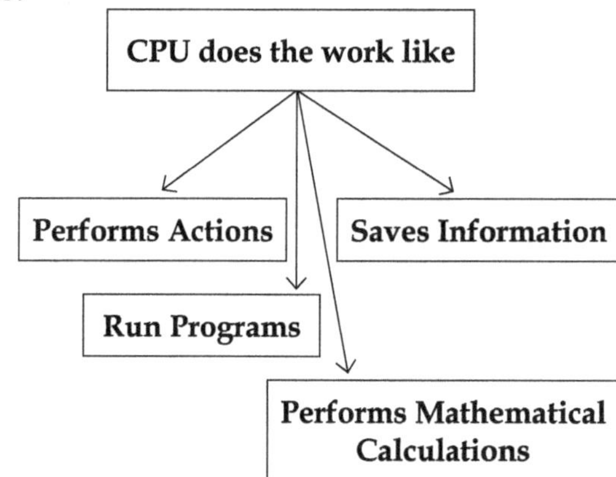

3. What are the parts of a computer?

Ans.

The main parts of a desktop computer are the monitor, CPU, keyboard, and mouse.

i. A monitor is a screen that helps us navigate on a computer. The movies we see or the games we play are all displayed on the monitor.

ii. Then comes the CPU or the Central Processing Unit. Like the human brain runs our entire body, similarly, the CPU runs the entire computer machine.

iii. Further, a keyboard is a rectangular board that contains all the keys that get used to play games. The keyboard lets us enter data into the computer and helps us navigate through it.

iv. Similar to a keyboard, a mouse is also used to navigate through the computer. It is also called a pointing device.

Apart from these main parts, there are also some additional parts that get used for different purposes. Like the printer, scanner, speakers, and microphones.

i. A printer is a device that lets us print what we see on the monitor.

ii. A scanner is basically a device that does the opposite of a printer. It helps us replicate what we see on paper to our monitor.

iii. Then come the speakers and microphones. When we connect speakers to a computer, we are able to hear the audio that the computer makes. When we connect microphones to a computer, we can send our voice into the computer.

All these devices are categorized into 2 sections – input devices and output devices.

Input devices are devices that help us send data into the computer whereas output devices are devices that help us receive data from the computer.

4. What is LCD & LED?

Ans.

Liquid Crystal Display (LCD) uses charged liquid crystals between two sheets of material such as glass or plastic to light up the proper pixels to form the image on the screen.

Light Emitting Diode (LED): A display that uses LED for the backlight is called an LED display. It consumes less power and is thinner, lighter and righter than LCD.

5. Why secondary storage devices are needed?

Ans.

Secondary storage devices are used to store large volume of data that exceed the capacity of main memory already present in the computer. It is non-volatile, persistent and not immediately accessible by a computer or processor. It allows users to store data and information that can be retrieved, transmitted, and used by apps and services quickly and easily.

Uses of Computer

4

Learning Objectives : In this chapter, students will learn about:

- ✓ At Home
- ✓ At Market
- ✓ At Banks
- ✓ At Other Places
- ✓ At School
- ✓ At Railway Stations and Airports
- ✓ At Hospitals

CHAPTER SUMMARY

Computer is an important part of human life nowadays. Computers are found almost everywhere from hospitals to schools to offices; We see computers in almost every field of our day-to-day life.

Let us explore the applications of computers in various fields and firstly at home.

At Home

At home we use a computer for:

- Drawing pictures
- Writing letters
- Playing games
- Listening to music
- Adding numbers
- Watching movies and cartoons

We have also seen our parents doing difficult calculations on computers, maintaining monthly expense records and buying things through the Internet on computers.

At School

At school, the first and the primary function of a computer is to teach students or to make learning their lessons more fun. Computers have made a huge impact on the teaching system. Teachers are using computers as a main tool for teaching core subjects. Teaching has become interactive through computers.

The other important functions of a computer in school are:

1. Supporting the admission procedure and preparing lists of students.
2. Maintaining fee records and attendance records of the students and teachers.
3. Preparing time-tables, worksheets and question papers.
4. Preparing result sheets.
5. In the school library, the computer helps maintain the records of the books.

At the Market

Whenever we visit a superstore or a multiplex, we see computers of different types. The main functions performed by them are:

1. They help in billing of the products.
2. They help in maintaining stock records of things in the shop.
3. In multiplexes, they help in printing tickets and flashing the name and timings of the movies.

At Railway Stations and Airports

Computers support the transport network immensely.

1. At railway stations and airports, it helps in ticketing and schedule maintenance.
2. Information on notice boards, flash train and flight timings are displayed on huge computer screens.
3. In the airport, there are specialised control rooms that manage the air flight routes through computers.
4. Computers help the hi-speed train drivers and the airplane pilots to track the route of the journey.

At Banks

Banks are another crucial place where computers are used widely.

1. Computers play an important role in maintenance of records of account holders and the money they have deposited in the bank.
2. Computers manage the cash withdrawal and the cash deposit.
3. They help in maintenance of the security system of the bank.
4. Every bank has a special facility called 'ATM' that is 'Automatic Teller Machine'. This machine helps the account holders to withdraw money instantly without visiting the bank.

At Hospitals

At hospitals,

1. Computers help maintain patient records.
2. They help in preparing medical and diagnostic reports.
3. Computerised devices help in detecting and even treating certain diseases.
4. Computers help maintain medicine stock records.

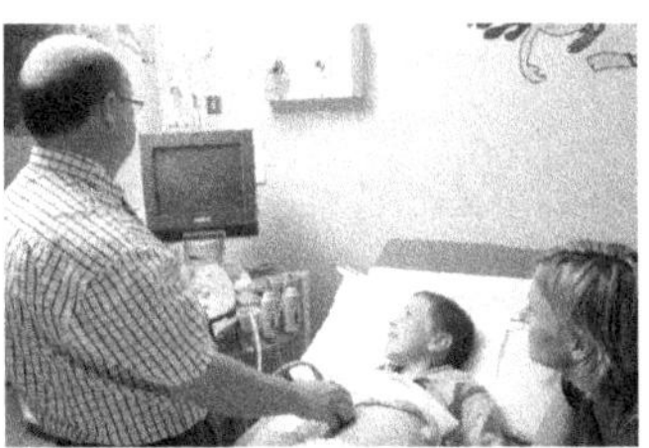

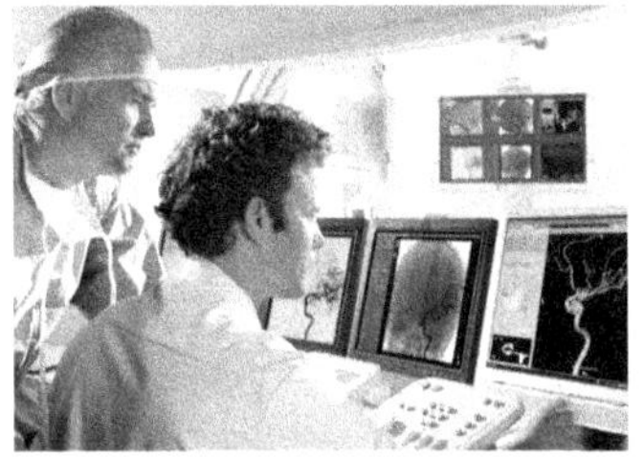

At Other Places

■ **Offices:** In offices, computers help in maintaining employee records, communication and mails and creating documents and files.

■ **Publishing industry:** In this industry, computers help in creating books and their designs. Computers help in printing and production of newspapers, too.

■ **Space station:** Advanced technology computers are used in space stations where they help in satellite and spacecraft launches and also monitor planetary activities in space.

■ **Entertainment industry:** Computers help in creating animation, movies, music and 3-D and advanced games.

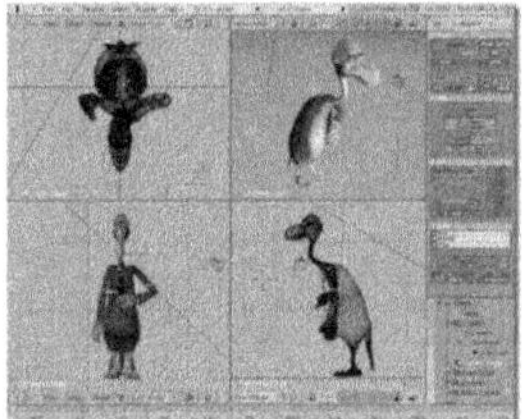

■ **Defence sector:** Computer technology is used to create advanced safety devices that enhance the defence powers of a country.

TRIVIA

The password of the computers in charge of controlling the nuclear missiles of the United States Army for years was 0000000000

➡ Computers help the hi-speed train drivers and the airplane pilots to track the route of the journey.

➡ Advanced technology computers are used in space stations where they help in satellite and spacecraft launches and also monitor planetary activities in space.

1. A school has computers at the following places
   (a) Library
   (b) Library and computer class
   (c) Library, school office and computer class
   (d) School office

2. At home we do not use computer for
   (a) Playing games
   (b) Washing clothes
   (c) Making projects
   (d) Watching movies

3. In a library, computers help in:
   (a) Maintaining salary records
   (b) Maintaining book records
   (c) Maintaining students performance records
   (d) Making test papers

4. In an office, computers

I. Make a task lengthy
II. Make employee attendance records
III. Make salary records
IV. Make working difficult

   (a) I only   (b) II and III
   (c) IV only   (d) I and IV

5. We find an ATM in
   (a) A bank
   (b) A space station
   (c) An office
   (d) A library

6. Philip is facing problems in deciding, which flight he should take to reach his brother's wedding on time. How will he get this information?
   (a) Philip will call in a bank; flight schedules are maintained in a dairy
   (b) Philip will call in a newspaper office; flight schedules are maintained in a newspaper
   (c) Philip will call an airport officer; flight schedules are maintained in a computer
   (d) Philip will call in a school library; flight schedules are maintained in a book

7. Which place is shown in the image below?

   (a) A library
   (b) A school
   (c) An office
   (d) A superstore

8. What is the person doing in the image shown below?

   (a) Withdrawing money from an ATM
   (b) Withdrawing money from a bank window
   (c) Submitting a book in a library
   (d) Taking out a ticket

9. In a space station, a computer
   (a) Monitors satellite positions
   (b) Monitors space activities and satellite positions
   (c) Monitors weather changes, space activities and satellite positions
   (d) Monitors flight schedules

10. Rehan has purchased lots of stuff from a shopping mall. What will the computer do now?
    (a) A computer will give him discount.
    (b) A computer will give him a certificate.
    (c) A computer will generate a bill.
    (d) A computer will give him money.

11. During the summer holidays, Saima and her friends went to a water park. At the water park they noticed computers. Tick the place where they could have seen computers:
    (a) At the ticket counter
    (b) At the swimming pool
    (c) At the water ride
    (d) In the costume room

12. Hemant has lost his library card. How could he find out the details?
    (a) He can ask the school teacher.
    (b) He can ask the librarian to check his computer data.
    (c) He can ask his friends.
    (d) He can ask his parents.

13. In a supermarket, there is a huge vegetable shop. The shop has 5 computers. What do the computers do there?

    | (I) | Keep vegetable stocks. |
    | (II) | Keep vegetable price list |
    | (III) | Keep customer name list |
    | (IV) | Store vegetables |

    (a) I only   (b) III only
    (c) I, II and III   (d) IV only

14. Which statement is true?
    (a) In a space station, a computer prints books.
    (b) In a school, a computer is used for playing games.
    (c) In a bank, a computer is used to maintain money records.
    (d) At home, computer is used to diagnose diseases.

15. In a hospital, where will you find a computer?
    (a) In hospital office
    (b) In the x-ray room
    (c) In the laboratory
    (d) All of the above

16. Which is not matched correctly?
    (a) Office-record keeping
    (b) Publishing-book designing
    (c) Entertainment-games making
    (d) Hospitals-watching movies

17. At an airport, what type of computer can we find?
    (a) Laptop
    (b) Desktop
    (c) Desktop and Mainframe computer
    (d) Tablets

18. Which of the following statements is incorrect for computers?
    (a) Computers have reduced the time taken to withdraw money from a bank account.
    (b) Computers have made learning an interesting process.
    (c) Computers create boring games.
    (d) Computers help in weather forecast.

19. In a village, we can find a computer at/in:
    (a) A post office
    (b) A bank
    (c) A police station
    (d) Every home

20. Who will not use a computer?
    (a) a cyclist
    (b) a pilot
    (c) a metro train driver
    (d) an astronaut

1. Read the following statements. How many are true?

    (I) Computers help maintain medicine stock records.

    (II) Computers help in flying air planes.

    (III) Computers help in running war tankers in war field.

    (IV) Computers help in evaluating test sheets.

    (a) I, II, III and IV (b) I and II

    (c) I and III (d) I and IV

2. In Airlines and Railways computer are used for tickets. Which one of the following is correct about the another use of computer in airlines and Railway?

    (a) Controlling the traffic

    (b) Updating the time table

    (c) Keeping records of passengers

    (d) All of these

3. Consider the following statements:

Statement 1: Better keyboard skill gives best productivity.
Statement 2: The upper row of the keyboard contains function keys.
Statement 3: The keyboard contain 26 alphabets keys

Which one of the following is correct about the above statements?

    (a) Statement 1 is true and 2 is false

    (b) Statement 1 is true

    (c) Statement 3 is true

    (d) All are correct

    (e) None of these

4. Marketing can be done over the internet. This is known as?

    (a) e-banking

    (b) e-marketing

    (c) e-business

    (d) e-books

5. Which device shown in the picture is used to project images from computer to a bigger screen?

    (a) Projector (b) Microphones

    (c) Speakers (d) Projector

1. Following are the pictures of some uses of computer. Look at the picture and write the name of the picture (its use) from the bracket given below:

Send e-mail, Watch a movie, Listen to music, Draw a picture, Chat with a friend, Play games, Type a document

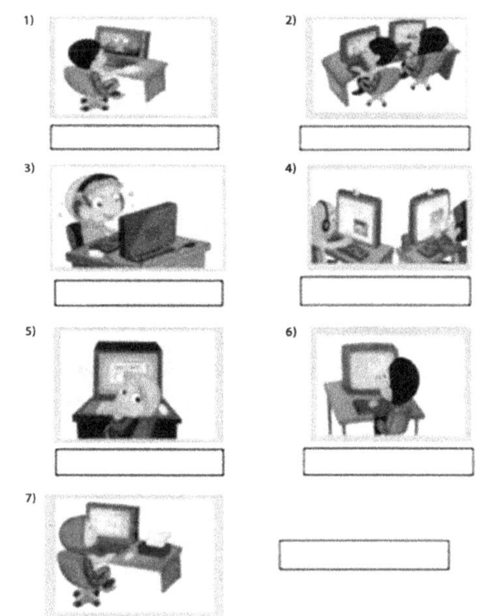

Ans.

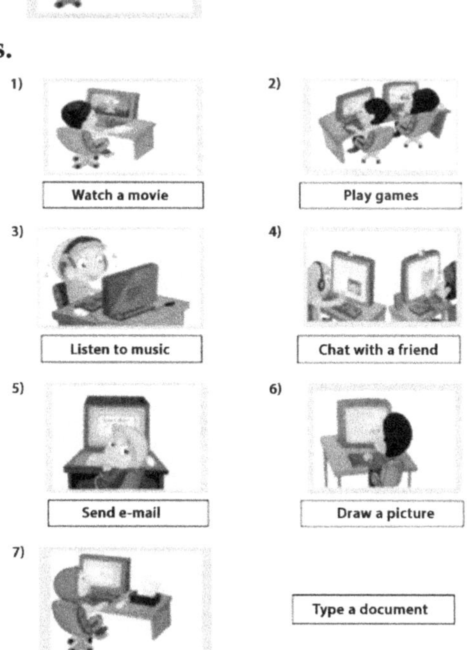

2. Where can computers be used?

Ans.

The functions of a computer are useful for people across all age groups, be it students like us, adults like our parents, or even elder adults like our grandparents. As such, computers can be seen almost everywhere. Some examples are at home where we use computers to watch movies, at a shop to simplify calculations, at banks to send emails, and at school to record attendance.

3. What is use of computers in a market?

Ans.

Whenever we visit a superstore or a multiplex, we see computers of different types. The main functions performed by them are:

i. They help in billing of the products.

ii. They help in maintaining stock records of things in the shop.

iii. In multiplexes, they help in printing tickets and flashing the name and timings of the movies.

4. What is the use of computers at Railway Stations and Airports?

Ans.

Computers support the transport network immensely:

i. At railway stations and airports, it helps in ticketing and schedule maintenance.

ii. Information on notice boards, flash train and flight timings are displayed on huge computer screens.

iii. In the airport, there are specialised control rooms that manage the air flight routes through computers.

iv. Computers help the hi-speed train drivers and the airplane pilots to track the route of the journey.

Learning to Use Keyboard   5

CHAPTER SUMMARY

The two main input devices of a computer are the keyboard and the mouse. These two devices transfer the information to the computer system.

Keyboard

Keyboard can be defined as a panel of keys used to input text or numbers into the computer. It consists of several keys like alphabet keys, numeral keys, function keys, space bar, escape key, arrow keys, functional keys, home key, end key, delete key, and many more. Each key has a specific function. There are around 104 keys on a standard keyboard.

Alphabet Keys

A-Z - Alphabet keys help in typing letters. In the latest keyboards, these letters are arranged in a QWERTY format. If you see the topmost row of the letters, you will locate the letters arranged in QWERTY sequence.

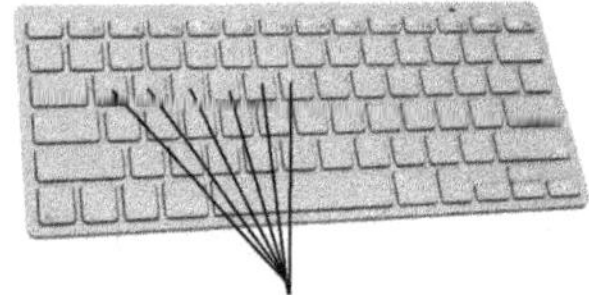

QWERTY Keyboard Alphabet Keys

Number Keys

Number keys help in typing numbers (0-9). There are two types of keyboards, one which has two set of number keys, and another that has only one set of number keys. The number pad present at the right hand side of the keyboard helps in carrying out fast typing and calculation of numbers.

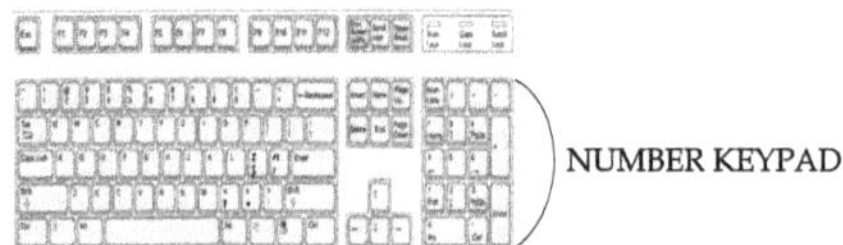

Symbol Keys

If we see the keyboard carefully, there are several symbols present on the keys. They are: !, @, $, &, (,), *, &, ^ , $, #, etc. These symbols can be typed by pressing the 'shift key' along with the 'symbol key', together.

- ■ Shift + 1 gives !
- ■ Shift +, gives <
- ■ Shift + a gives A (when the Caps Lock is off)
- ■ Shift + A gives a (when the Caps Lock is on)
- ■ Shift + 3 gives #, and many others.

Symbol Key

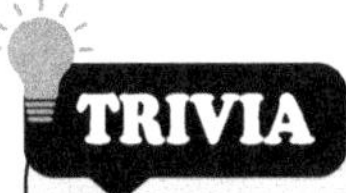

You can spell the word typewriter using the top line of letters on a computer's keyboard.

Function Keys

These keys are 12 in number and are located at the top of a keyboard. They provide special instructions to a computer to carry out certain actions quickly. For example, pressing F1 when using a Windows program will allow a user to access the Help screen.

Navigation Key

There are four navigation keys in a keyboard. These keys help in moving the cursor that blinks on the monitor screen to move in four respective directions, left, right, up and down. The other navigation keys are Home and End key. Home key when pressed moves the cursor to the starting point of the line in which the cursor is blinking, whereas the End key moves the cursor to the end of the line.

Special Keys

There are several special keys on a keyboard that carry out specific functions to facilitate functioning of the keyboard.

These are:

1. Backspace Key
2. Delete Key
3. CTRL and ALT keys
4. Shift Key
5. Enter Key
6. Esc key
7. Tab Key
8. Caps lock key
9. Page up and Page down keys
10. Space bar

Backspace key: This key helps in deleting text backwards. It is generally used while typing letters, preparing projects, etc. It helps in making corrections.

Delete key: This is also a text deletion key. It deletes text in forward direction (the text on the right side of the cursor).

CTRL and ALT key: These keys are used in coordination with other keys to carry out specific functions.

For example: 'CTRL' and 'S' if pressed together, will save the document on which you are working.

Shift key: This key is also used in coordination with another key. They are generally used to type symbols and capital letters (in case caps lock is 'off').

For example: Shift + a gives A (when the Caps Lock is off).

Enter key: When we write a letter or a story, pressing the Enter key moves the cursor to the next line.

Esc key: This key helps stop or cancel a command.

Tab key: This key moves the cursor ahead to a particular distance. Tab key is also used in coordination with another key to carry out specific functions.

Caps Lock Key: This is a special key which if pressed will help in typing letters in capital.

For example: e → Caps Lock ON → E

Page Up and Page Down key: These keys help in navigating page wise. For example, if we have a long word file to read, we can use Page UP and Down file to scroll across the document.

Space Bar: It is the longest key on the keyboard. It helps in giving space between words and text. When we press this key, the cursor moves one point ahead on the screen.

➡ Keyboard can be defined as a panel of keys used to input text or numbers into the computer.

➡ Number keys help in typing numbers (0-9). There are two types of keyboards, one which has two set of number keys, and another that has only one set of number keys.

➡ These keys are 12 in number and are located at the top of a keyboard.

1. Alphabet keys have
   (a) 1, 2, 3   (b) B, T, g, a, s, D
   (c) @, $, ^, *,)   (d) A, D, R, E, T

2. A shift key is used for
   (a) It is used to type numbers.
   (b) It is used in association with other keys to type symbols and capital letters.
   (c) It is used to type capital letters.
   (d) It is used to type symbols.

3. The number pad has the following series of numbers
   (a) 0-9   (b) 1-10
   (c) 1-20   (d) 1-100

4. Which set of keys is shown in the image below?

   (a) Symbol   (b) Alphabet
   (c) Number   (d) Function

5. This is not a special key.
   (a) A, B, C   (b) CTRL
   (c) Shift key   (d) Alt

6. Read the statement below. Which key will you use to make the correction?

   An elephant is eating grass.
   (a) Home key   (b) Backspace key
   (c) Delete key   (d) Enter key

7. This is the longest key on the keyboard.
   (a) Enter   (b) CTRL
   (c) Space bar   (d) Function

8. Match the following correctly:

I		II
(i) Alphabet key	(a)	! @ #
(ii) Shift key	(b)	F9 F10
(iii) Symbol Key	(c)	A S D
(iv) Function Key	(d)	⇧ Shift

   (a) i-a, ii-b, iii-c, iv-d
   (b) i-c, ii-d, iii-a, iv-b
   (c) i-d, ii-c, iii-b, iv-a
   (d) i-c, ii-a, iii-d, iv-b

9. An * will be typed with the help of
   (a) Shift key   (b) Ctrl key
   (c) 8 no. key   (d) Shift + 8

10. Rohit is on page 13 of a computer file, he wants to read a story on page 15. Which key will he use?
    (a) Backspace
    (b) Upward navigation key
    (c) Page Down
    (d) Page Up

11. Meena opened a program by mistake. She is unable to close it. What will she do?
    (a) She will press CTRL
    (b) She will press Esc
    (c) She will press Del
    (d) She will press Tab

12. A Caps Lock key of a keyboard is not functional. Which key would you use to type capital letters?
    (a) Shift key + Alphabet
    (b) Tab key + Alphabet
    (c) Number key + Alphabet
    (d) Ctrl key + Alphabet

13. Which keys will you use to type numbers quickly?
    (a) We will use the separate number keys at the right hand side of the key board.
    (b) We will press the Num lock and then use the separate number keypad at the right hand side.
    (c) We will use the horizontal number line on the top of the alphabets.
    (d) We will press Caps Lock and then use the separate number keypad at the right hand side.

14. What will happen when we use the following keys together?

Shift + test

(a) It will type: %^^&*
(b) It will type TEST
(c) It will type test
(d) It will type 1234

15. Which key will you use to move to the last position in a row?

(a) Insert   (b) Home
(c) Delete   (d) End

16. Match the following correctly.

Key	Output
(i) Shift + R (caps lock off)	(a) B
(ii) Caps Lock + b	(b) 12345
(iii) Shift + 7	(c) R
(iv) Num Lock + 12345	(d) &

(a) i-c, ii-a, iii-d, iv-b
(b) i-c, ii-b, iii-d, iv-a
(c) i-c, ii-d, iii-a, iv-b
(d) i-d, ii-a, iii-c, iv-b

17. Which set has all special keys in it?

(a) Shift, alphabet, number
(b) Shift, ctrl, number
(c) Shift, F1, Tab
(d) Alphabet, number, backspace

18. What is the pattern of the alphabet keys on the keyboard?

(a) ABCD   (b) QWTY
(c) ASDFB   (d) QWERTY

19. Match the following correctly.

Key	Function
(i) Shift ⇧	(a) helps type capital alphabets
(ii) ←	(b) moves the cursor to the starting of the row
(iii) |Home|	(c) special key helps in typing symbols
(iv) Caps Lock	(d) navigates the cursor to left

(a) i-c, ii-b, iii-d, iv-a
(b) i-c, ii-a, iii-b, iv-d
(c) i-a, ii-d, iii-b, iv-c
(d) i-c, ii-d, iii-b, iv-a

20. What is wrong in the keyboard below?

(a) The number pad on the right is wrong.
(b) The alphabet key should be A, B, C, D in sequence.
(c) The symbol keys should be separate.
(d) The numbers should range from 1-10.

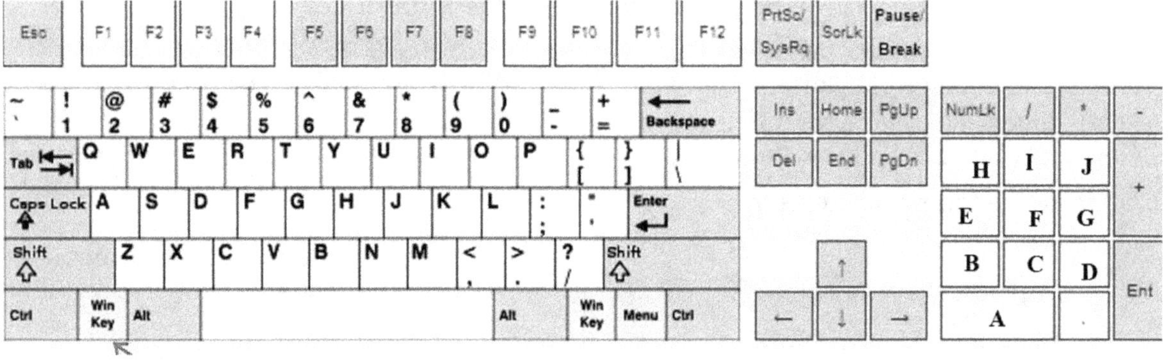

1. The function of  are same in case we want to
   - (a) Type a capital letter Y
   - (b) Type d
   - (c) Type @
   - (d) Type >

2. Which key will you use to close this function?

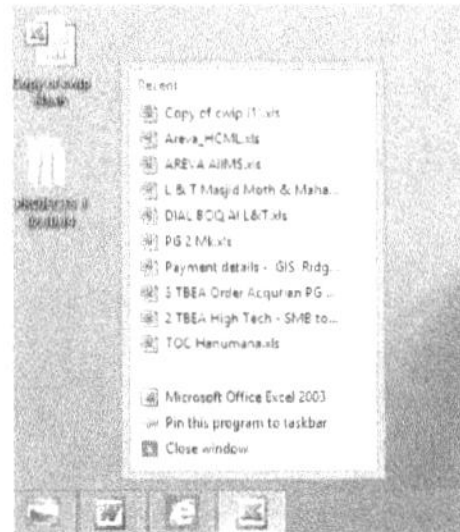

   (a) F1
   (b) Print Screen SysRq
   (c) Backspace
   (d) Esc

3. Small led light on the keyboard tells us capslock key is
   - (a) ON / OFF
   - (b) ON / ON
   - (c) OFF / OFF

4. Common between a keyboard, mobile, casio, calculator are.
   - (a) keys
   - (b) style
   - (c) size

5. The given device is of which type?
   - (a) Input
   - (b) Output
   - (c) Both input and output
   - (d) None of these

1. Join the following keyboard keys pictures with their names:

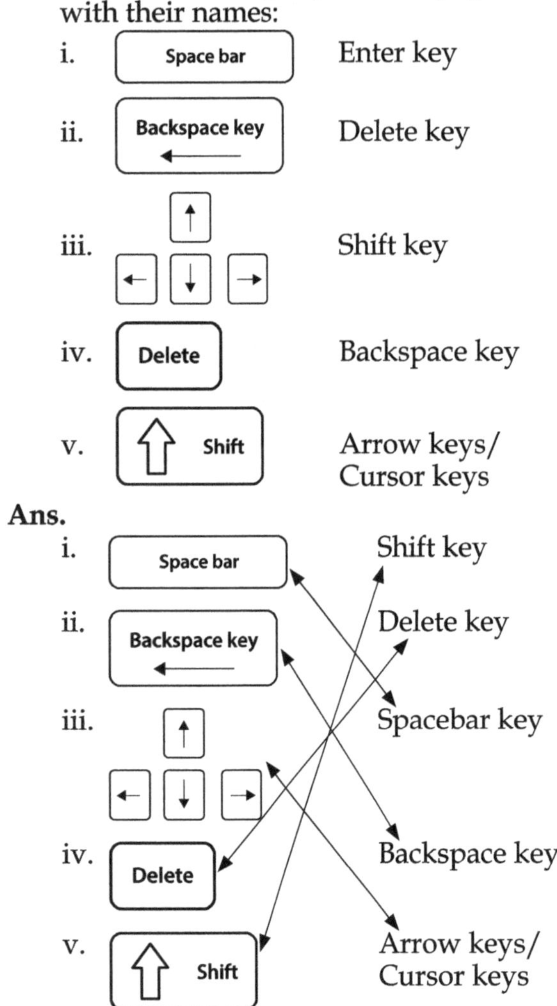

2. Fill in the blanks by choosing the correct option from the bracket:

(Spacebar key, Enter key, Number keys, Alphabet keys, Backspace key)

i. We can type letters while entering information or data into the computer are by using __________.

ii. We can move our cursor to the next new line by using __________.

iii. The __________ is used for adding a blank space between the selected characters or words.

iv. The __________ on the keyboard is used for erasing the selected characters from right side of the cursor to the left.

v. This __________ is used for entering numbers into the computer.

Ans.

i. We can type letters while entering information or data into the computer are by using <u>Alphabet keys</u>.

ii. We can move our cursor to the next new line by using <u>Enter key</u>.

iii. The <u>Spacebar key</u> is used for adding a blank space between the selected characters or words.

iv. The <u>Backspace key</u> on the keyboard is used for erasing the selected characters from right side of the cursor to the left.

v. This <u>Number keys</u> is used for entering numbers into the computer.

Learning to Use Mouse

Learning Objectives : In this chapter, students will learn about:
- ✓ Mouse
- ✓ Types of Mouse
- ✓ Functioning of a Mouse

CHAPTER SUMMARY

Mouse

A mouse is an input device with an interesting shape. It resembles a mouse hence is named so. The shape is designed so as it fits into our palm easily. The arrow that appears on the computer monitor indicates the presence of a mouse. It is known as a Cursor or Pointer or Arrow. The pointer helps us to play games, draw pictures and select a file on the desktop.

Types of Mouse

A mouse has two main buttons: a left button and a right button. The left button is used the most. In the centre of a mouse is a scroll wheel or in some, there is a third button at the centre that acts as a scroll wheel. The scroll wheel, between the buttons helps us move up or down through documents easily.

Some advanced mouse devices have additional buttons that can perform other functions.

There are different types of mouse available in the market.

Three-buttoned mouse: It has three buttons with the central button acting as a scroll wheel.

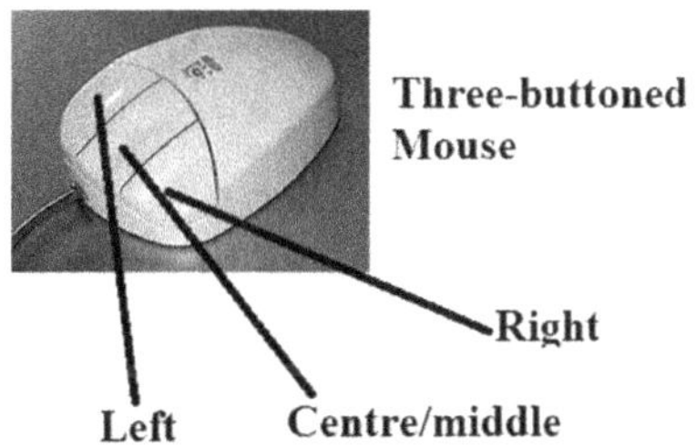

Two-buttoned mouse: It has only two buttons.

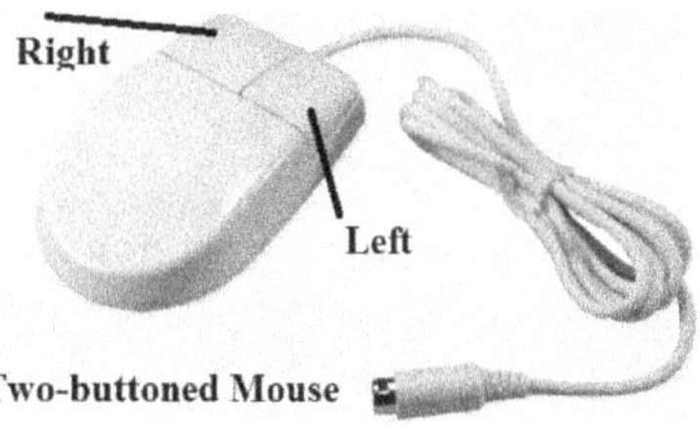

Scroll mouse: A scroll mouse has a circular wheel on top of the mouse in between the left and the right button.

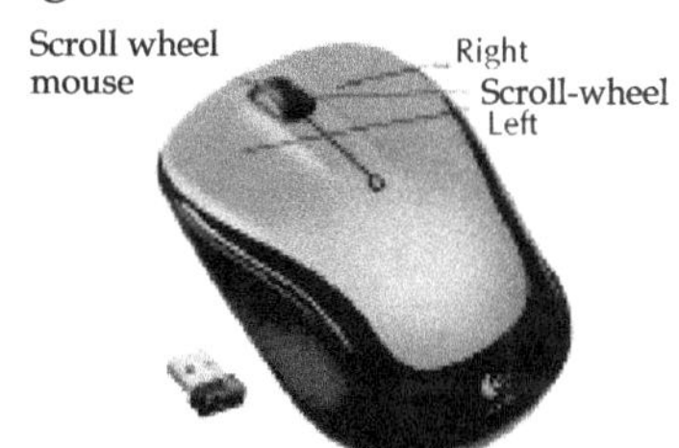

Ball mouse: A ball mouse has a ball type rubber roller at the base of the mouse. It helps in moving the mouse cursor on the monitor screen. This type of mouse requires a soft-padded base on which it can move, mostly referred to as the mouse pad.

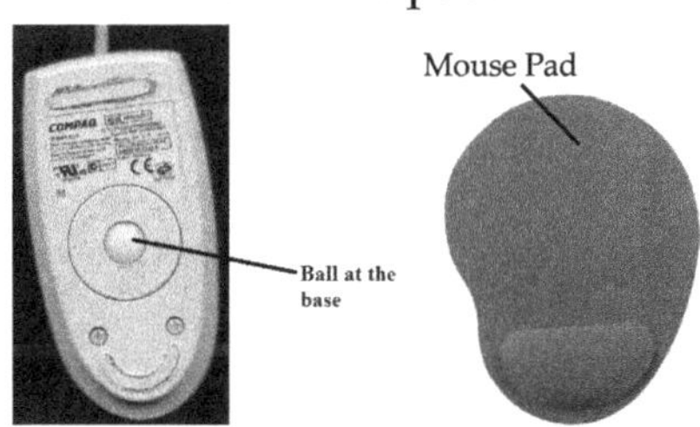

The first computer mouse was made of Wood.

Laser/optical mouse: This mouse has a light blinking at the base or on the mouse body that shows the movement of the cursor on the monitor screen. Mostly, these mouse devices are wireless and they are connected to the computer through a small device.

Actions of a Mouse

It is important to know the actions performed by the left and the right buttons of the mouse.

The four main actions of a mouse are:

- Left single click
- Left double click
- Right click
- Drag and drop

Left single click: The pressing of left button once is left single click. This helps in selecting an item (icon, file, folder).

Left double click: Pressing the left button twice is left double click. This action helps in executing an action, for example, there is a game icon on the desktop screen, we can open that game by double clicking on that icon.

Right click: This action is used to open a list of commands that can be executed.

Drag and Drop: In this action, the left mouse button is kept pressed and the selected item is moved from one place to another by manually moving the mouse. When the mouse button is released, the item which has been moved from position A to position B remains at position B.

Other types of input devices similar to mouse are:

Joystick: used to play games.

Stylus pen: used for touch screen computers and tablets.

Trackball mouse: a small ball that is set in a holder and can be rotated by hand to move a cursor on a computer screen.

- A mouse is an input device with an interesting shape.
- A scroll mouse has a circular wheel on top of the mouse in between the left and the right button.
- Pressing the left button twice is left double click. This action helps in executing an action.

1. A mouse is a
    (a) Tracking device
    (b) An input device
    (c) An output device
    (d) A processing device

2. A mouse is connected with
    (a) A monitor
    (b) A CPU
    (c) A UPS
    (d) A switch board

3. Tick the wrong group.
    (a) Two-buttoned mouse, three-buttoned mouse
    (b) Three-buttoned mouse, scroll mouse
    (c) Scroll mouse, five button mouse
    (d) Laser mouse, Ball mouse

4. What is the slant arrow that represents the mouse on the monitor screen?
    (a) Mouse pointer   (b) Cursor
    (c) Keyword   (d) Line

5. This moves when the mouse is moved manually.
    (a) Icon   (b) Files
    (c) Desktop   (d) Cursor

6. This is not a mouse action.
    (a) Drag and drop   (b) Refresh
    (c) Right click   (d) Left click

7. This term is not related to a mouse.
    (a) Laser   (b) Ball
    (c) Drag   (d) Keys

8. Mehul wants to open a picture on his desktop, what will he do?
    (a) He will double left click on the picture icon present on the desktop.
    (b) He will drag the picture present on the desktop.
    (c) He will right click on the picture and then drag it.
    (d) He will left click, once on the picture.

9. Match the following correctly.

Mouse action name		Function
(a) Right click	(i)	Moves an item from one place to another on the desktop
(b) Left single click	(ii)	Opens the list of commands
(c) Left double click	(iii)	Executes a function or opens a file or program
(d) Drag and Drop	(iv)	Selects an item on the desktop

    (a) a-iii, b-iv, c-ii, d-i
    (b) a-ii, b-iv, c-iii, d-i
    (c) a-iv, b-ii, c-iii, d-i
    (d) a-ii, b-iv, c-i, d-iii

10. Observe the image below. What is happening in the image?

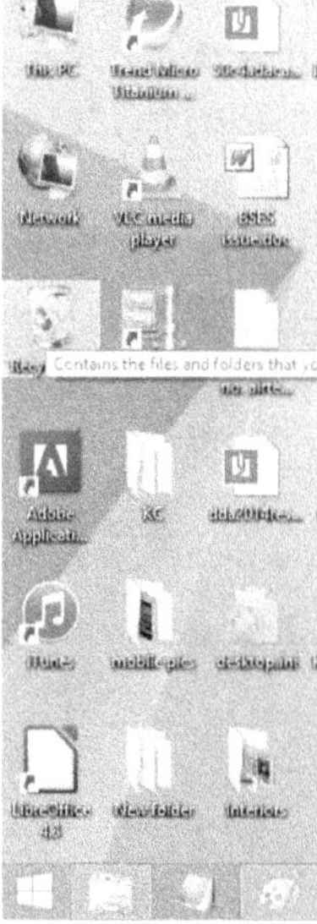

    (a) The mouse has dragged the icon.
    (b) The mouse has single left clicked the icon.
    (c) The mouse has opened the icon.
    (d) The mouse has right clicked on the icon.

11. The central wheel of a mouse is known as ____________.
    (a) Trackball   (b) Rubber ball
    (c) Scroll wheel   (d) Trackwheel

12. A ball mouse needs a ________ for support and movement.
    (a) Mouse pad   (b) CPU
    (c) Monitor   (d) UPS

13. Which part of the body do we use while using our mouse?
    (a) Upper limbs
    (b) Lower limbs
    (c) Pelvic region
    (d) Abdominal region

14. Some mouse devices have a light blinking on them. What is it?
    (a) An electrical source
    (b) A battery symbol
    (c) A laser light
    (d) A scroll wheel indicator

15. To complete an action of a mouse, we will
    (a) Right click it
    (b) We will double left click it
    (c) We will drag and drop
    (d) We will single left click

16. Which finger is used the most while using a mouse?
    (a) Middle finger
    (b) Index finger
    (c) Thumb
    (d) Smallest finger

17. This is not a pointing device.

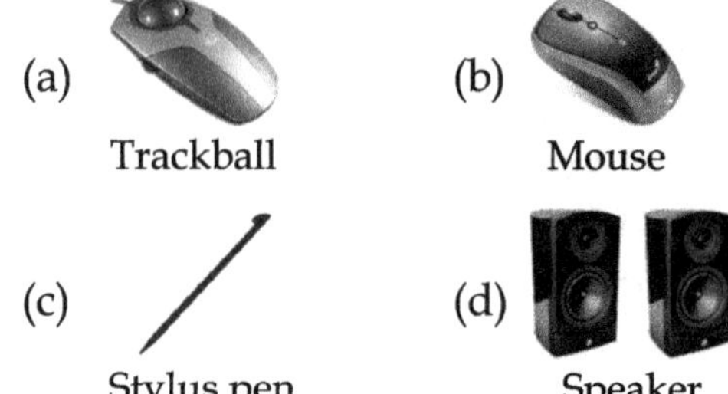

    (a) Trackball   (b) Mouse
    (c) Stylus pen   (d) Speaker

18. Find the odd one out.

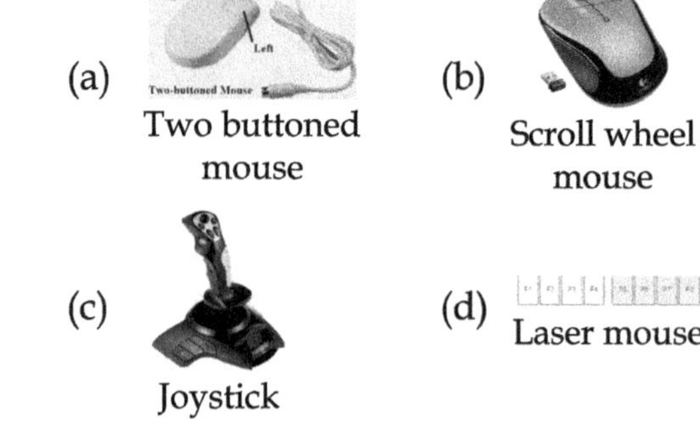

    (a) Two buttoned mouse   (b) Scroll wheel mouse
    (c) Joystick   (d) Laser mouse

19. One of the following statements is false.
    (a) A mouse helps in playing games.
    (b) A mouse stores data.
    (c) A mouse helps in selecting a file.
    (d) A mouse may or may not have a connecting wire.

20. Mohit is organising icons on his desktop. Which mouse function will he use?
    (a) Drag and Drop
    (b) Right click
    (c) Left Click
    (d) Dragging the mouse

1. Sachin wants to place the Recycle Bin icon at the topmost left corner of his desktop screen, How will he do this?

    (a) He will use double click action of the mouse.

    (b) He will use delete button of the keyboard.

    (c) He will use drag and drop function of the mouse.

    (d) He will right click on the icon.

2. I. Identify the following image.

    II. What will happen when you move your mouse cursor over it?

	I	II
(a)	Menu Bar	a menu will open
(b)	Taskbar	a small preview window is flashed
(c)	Menu Bar	a file will open
(d)	Taskbar	a list of items will be shown

3. What is happening in the image below?

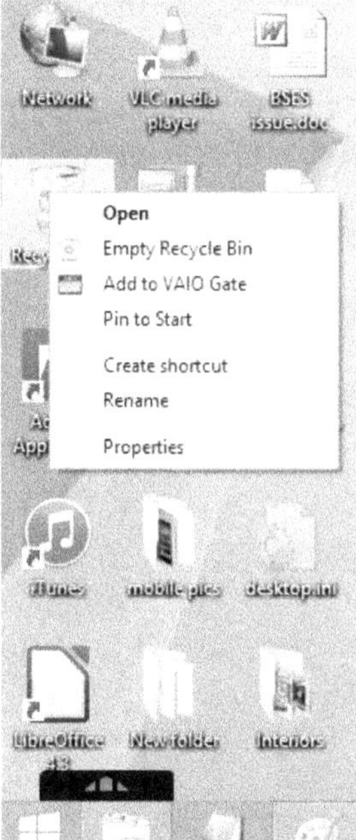

    (a) The computer mouse has double clicked on the Recycle Bin icon.

    (b) The computer mouse has right clicked on the Recycle Bin icon.

    (c) The computer mouse has left clicked on the Recycle Bin icon.

    (d) The computer mouse has dragged the Recycle Bin icon.

4. The word 'Mouse' is very much popular in computer world. The word 'Mouse' is originated at the

    (a) Stanford Research Institute

    (b) American Research Institute

    (c) Spanish Research Institute

    (a) Cambridge Research

5. The _______ of the mouse pointer changes according to the task and application.

    (a) style   (b) colour

    (c) shape   (d) size

1. Following are the pictures of some uses Label the computer mouse given below using the words from the brackets:

Left button, Scroll Wheel, Cable wire, Right button, Button, Mouse pad

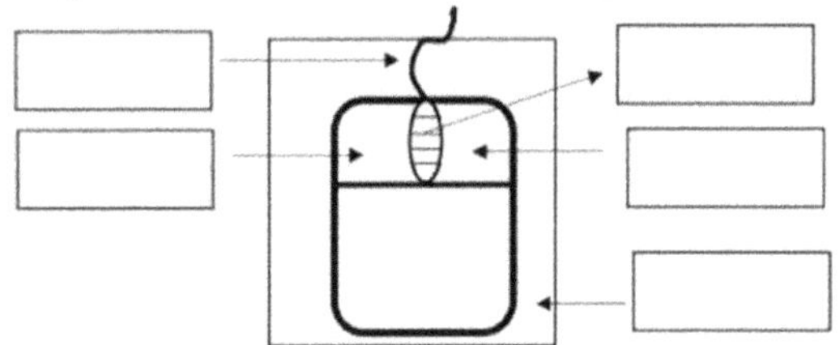

Ans.

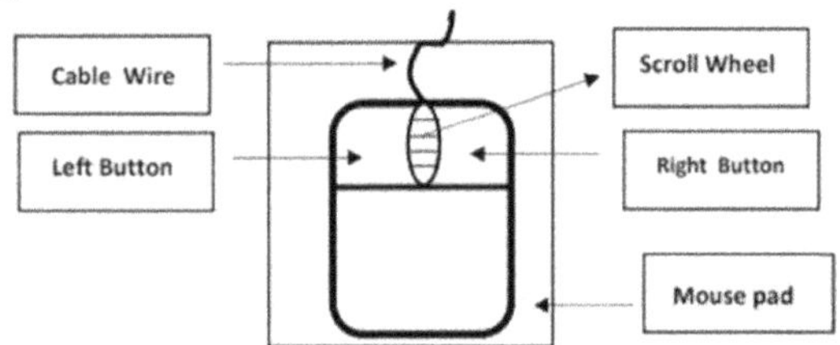

2. Fill in the blanks by selecting the correction option from the brackets:

   (a) Mouse is connected to the CPU with the long ________ (Tape, Wire)

   (b) Mouse is an ____ device. (Input, Output)

   (c) The pressing of mouse button is called as ____ (Clicking, Touching)

   (d) Mouse is also known as ________ device. (Rat, Pointing or Clicking)

   (e) Every mouse has ____ or ____ buttons on it. (two or three, ten)

Ans.

   (a) Mouse is connected to the CPU with the long Wire.

   (b) Mouse is an Input device.

   (c) The pressing of mouse button is called as Clicking.

   (d) Mouse is also known as Pointing or Clicking device.

   (e) Every mouse has two or three buttons on it.

3. Write Right or Wrong against the statement given below:

   (a) Mouse is an Output device. ________

   (b) Mouse is connected to the CPU with a long wire. ________

   (c) Rat is the other name of a mouse. ________

   (d) Mouse has one button on it. ________

   (e) Mouse is used to draw pictures in Paint. ________

Ans.

   (a) Mouse is an Output device. **Wrong**

   (b) Mouse is connected to the CPU with a long wire. **Right**

   (c) Rat is the other name of a mouse. **Wrong**

   (d) Mouse has one button on it. **Wrong**

   (e) Mouse is used to draw pictures in Paint. **Right**

4. Complete the following sentences with the help of the words given in the brackets:

   (Input device, Arrow pointer, Drawing, playing, long wire, Clicking)

   A mouse is an ________ It is connected to the CPU with the help of a ________ the white colour arrow that you see on your monitor screen is called as ________ We make use of for ________ pictures and ________ games. We can easily open any file, program or folder by just simply pointing the Arrow pointer on it, and ________ it.

Ans.

   A mouse is an input device. It is connected to the CPU with the help of a long wire. The white colour arrow that you see on your monitor screen is called as arrow pointer. We make use of mouse for drawing pictures and playing games. We can easily open any file, program or folder by just simply pointing the Arrow pointer on it and clicking it.

Learning Objectives : In this chapter, students will learn about:
- ✓ MS Paint – A Colourful Software
- ✓ Opening MS Paint
- ✓ Components of a Paint Window

CHAPTER SUMMARY

MS Paint – A Colourful Software

Computer has an operating system (a system which helps in functioning of the computer) called **Windows**. Windows has many applications in it. One of them is MS Paint. MS Paint is a drawing tool that helps us to create pictures and drawings on the computer. MS Paint is a very practical application, the more you use it, the more you will learn about it.

The MS Paint icon on Windows looks like this:

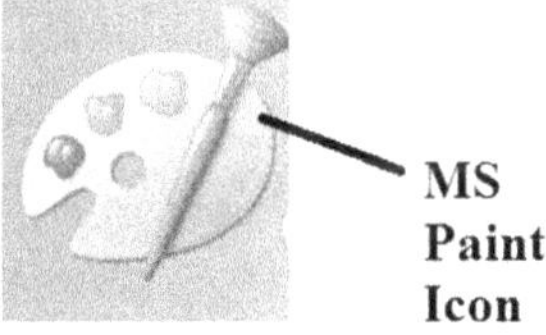

MS
Paint
Icon

And the graphical user interface with which you can do the work on the software looks like the following image:

Opening MS Paint

The MS Paint application can be opened as follows:

- Click on the Start Menu.
- Click on "All Programs" option.

- Point the cursor on "Accessories."
- Select "Paint" from the sub menu and double left click on it.

If the given icon is present on the desktop, then with the help of a mouse, we can double click on the icon and open the application directly.

Components of a Paint Window

The main components of the Paint application are: Title bar, Menu bar, Quick access tool bar, ribbon and drawing area.

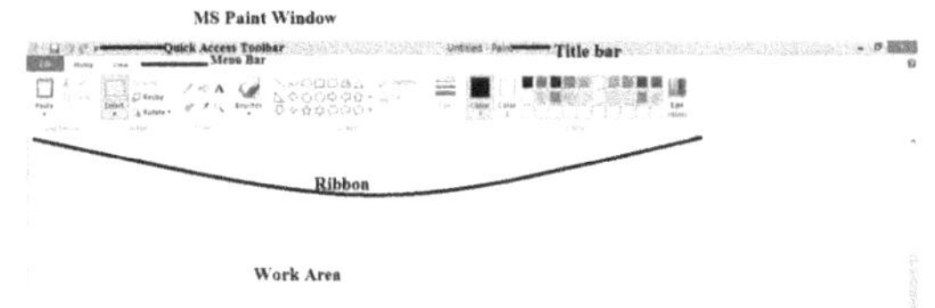

Title Bar: The title bar is the topmost bar. This bar possesses the name of the file; a blank new file is generally titled 'Untitled-Paint'. The title bar also has the Quick Access toolbar placed on it at the left hand side of the window. The title bar contains minimise, maximise, restore, move, resize and close buttons on it.

Menu Bar: has three main tabs on it, file, home and view.

Quick Access Toolbar: The most important buttons of a Quick Access Toolbar are: Save, Redo and Undo. We can add buttons to the Quick Access Toolbar as per our requirement.

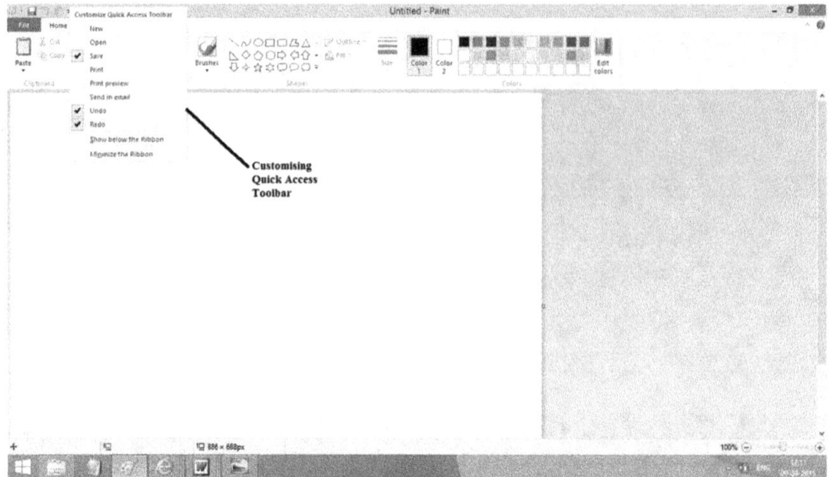

Ribbon: There are several heads/tabs under the ribbon. These tabs possess specific functions. They are:

(a) **Clipboard tab:** It has paste, cut and copy buttons in it.

(b) **Image tab:** This tab has components like, select, resize, rotate and crop. All these buttons help in making changes to the picture or the drawing. The select tool helps in selecting a particular shape of area of the picture. It has a sub-menu.

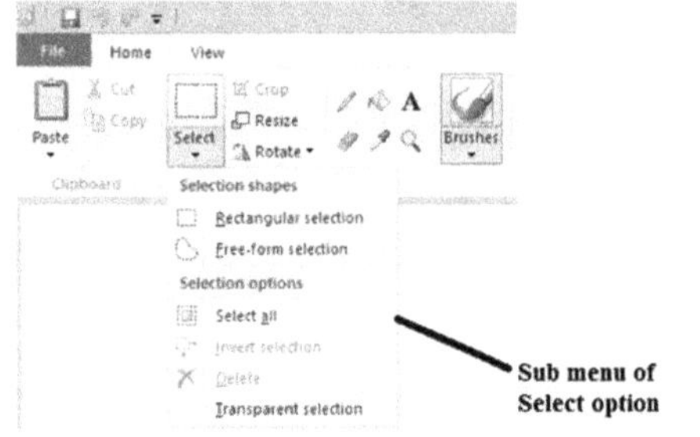

Similarly, the rotate button also has a sub-menu.

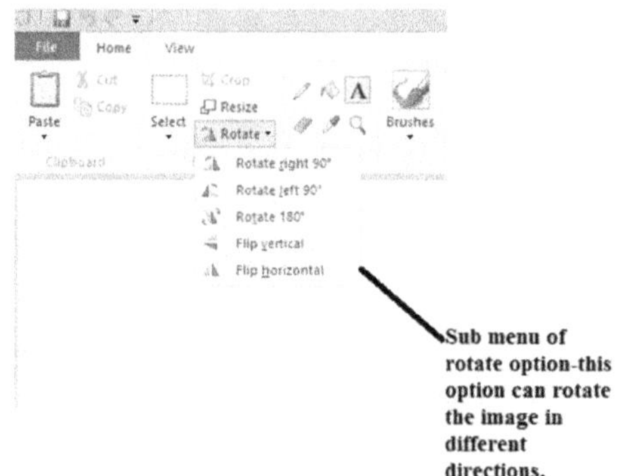

(c) **Tools tab:** It has various buttons like: pencil tool (for free hand drawing), erase tool, fill colour tool, colour picker, magnifier and text tool. If we move our mouse cursor over a particular tool, the MS Paint software will flash its use and purpose in a box.

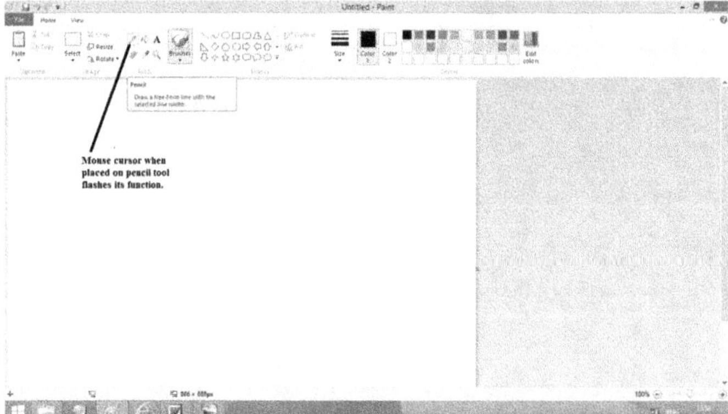

The size of the eraser can also be increased by a shortcut command: Ctrl+ '+' button on the Numpad.

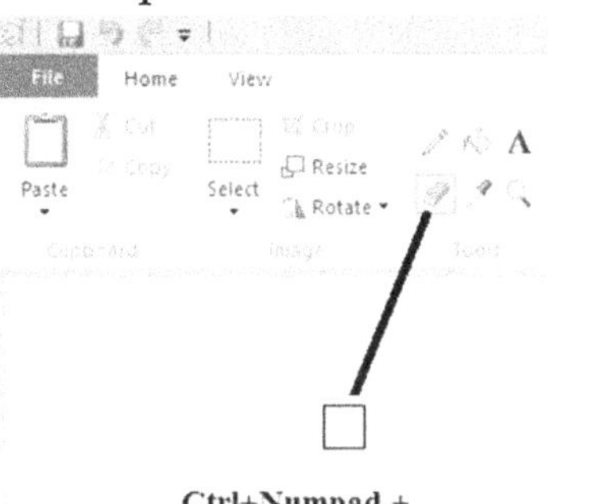

Ctrl+Numpad +

(d) **Shapes and Brushes tab:** MS paint provides several shapes and brush styles.

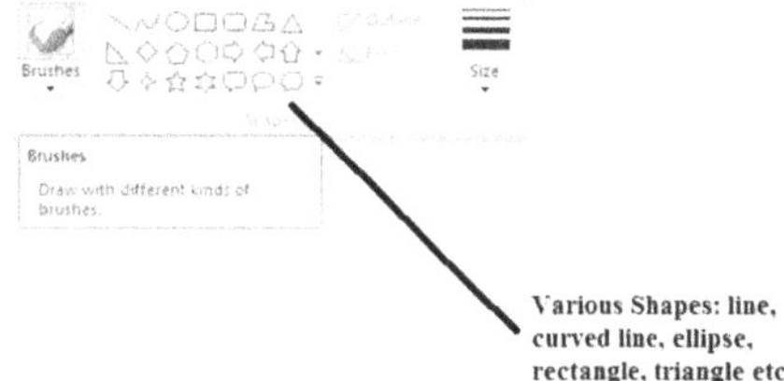

While using the elliptical shape, if we want to draw a perfect circle, we can press the Shift key, while dragging the mouse and drawing the circle.

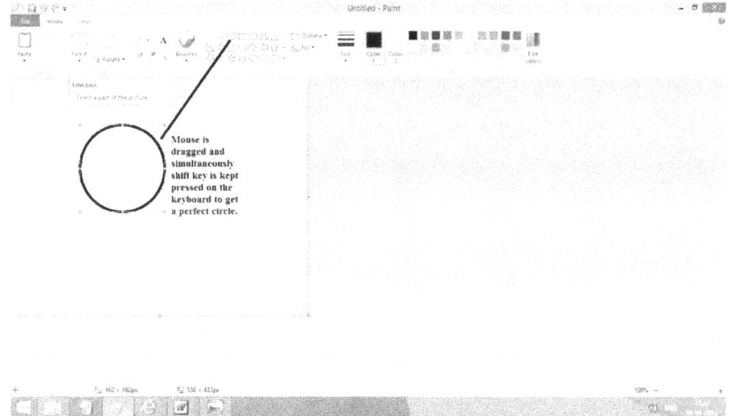

(e) **Colour palette:** The colour palette helps us to select various colours of our choice.

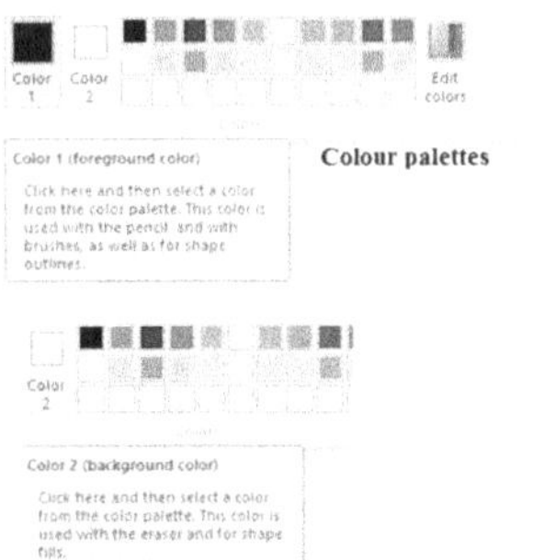

TRIVIA

The original Paint program boasts more than 100 million monthly users.

MUST REMEMBER

➡ MS Paint is a drawing tool that helps us to create pictures and drawings on the computer.

1. What is MS Paint?
   (a) A writing tool
   (b) A drawing tool
   (c) A gaming tool
   (d) A music tool

2. When you open a new paint file, what appears on the title bar?
   (a) Untitled-Paint
   (b) 1-Paint
   (c) New-Paint
   (d) First-Paint

3. Where is quick access toolbar located?
   (a) It is located above the title bar.
   (b) It is located vertically on the left side
   (c) It is located on the left side of the title bar.
   (d) It is located in the ribbon.

4. Which tool helps us draw free-form drawing?
   (a) [pencil icon]   (b) **A**
   (c) [line icon]   (d) [brushes icon]
   Brushes

5. Which tool is part of the shapes window?
   (a) [magnifier icon]   (b) **A**
   (c) [oval icon]   (d) [fill icon]

6. Which colour button will you use for foreground colour?
   (a) Color 1   (b) Color 2
   (c) Edit colors   (d) Brushes

7. We cannot fill colour in a
   (a) Circle   (b) Rectangle
   (c) Star   (d) Curved line

8. We can have a colour spray effect with this tool.
   (a) [icon]   (b) [icon]
   (c) [icon]   (d) 

9. Observe the image below and tick the correct set of tools used to get this image.

   (a) Line tool
   (b) Line and brush tool
   (c) Line tool and size tool
   (d) Line tool and pencil tool

10. What is the difference between I and II?

   I   II

   (a) Image I is made by line tool and image II by pencil.
   (b) Image I is rotated to 90° to get image II.
   (c) Image I and II has no difference.
   (d) Image I has longer lines than image II.

11. Both the following tools belong to

   ✕ <u>D</u>elete   ⬚ <u>R</u>ectangular selection

   (a) Shapes tab
   (b) Colors tab
   (c) Brushes tab
   (d) Selection button

12. The following image could be produced using spray can?

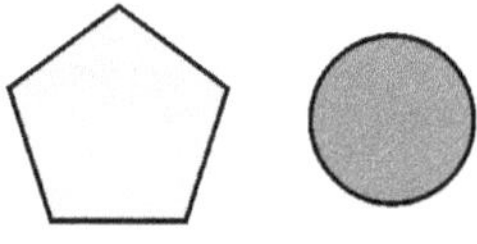

   (a) Shape tool, brush tool, line tool and colour
   (b) Shapes, colour and colour fill
   (c) Shape tool, line tool and colour
   (d) Shape tool, colour fill, line tool and colour

13. Which is the best suited answer for the following question? Define select tool.
    (a) Selects a part of a picture
    (b) Selects the complete picture
    (c) Selects a rectangular or free form part of the picture
    (d) Can select, rectangular or free form shape of the picture or the entire picture.

14. Mohit has created an image of a flower, but when he took its printout, the image was very small in size. Which tool will he use to increase the image size?
    (a) Select and rotate
    (b) Select and resize
    (c) Select and crop
    (d) Resize

15. Look at the images shown below. Which is labelled incorrectly?

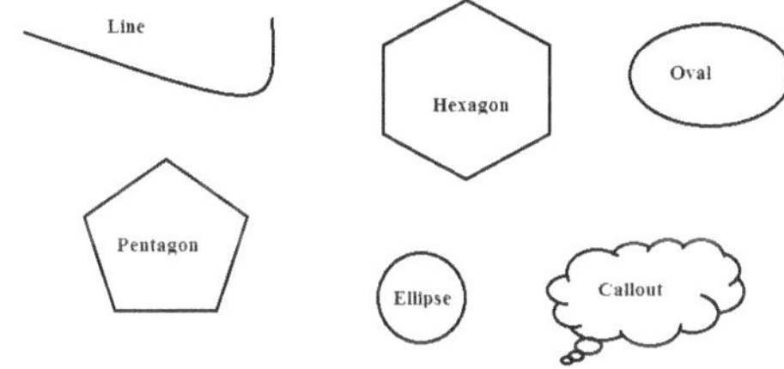

    (a) Line, ellipse and call out
    (b) Line and ellipse
    (c) Ellipse
    (d) Call out and ellipse

16. What is this area?

    (a) Quick access toolbar
    (b) Ribbon
    (c) Clipboard in Ribbon
    (d) Editing tools

17. Match the following correctly.

Tool		Function	
(a) 		(i)	Polygon shape
(b)		(ii)	Flip the picture or selection
(c) Rotate		(iii)	Erase part of the picture
(d)		(iv)	Star shape

    (a) a-ii, b-iii, c-iv, d-i
    (b) a-iii, b-ii, c-iv, d-i
    (c) a-ii, b-iii, c-i, d-iv
    (d) a-iii, b-iv, c-ii, d-i

18. Under which head can we open a new paint file?
    (a) Home tab
    (b) Quick access toolbar
    (c) Quick access toolbar or File Menu
    (d) File menu

19. Amita wants to create the following image, how will she do it?

    (a) She will use shapes.
    (b) She will use shapes, cut and copy button.
    (c) She will use shapes and copy, and paste repeatedly.
    (d) She will use shapes and copy.

20. How many styles of brushes are there?
    (a) 8   (b) 10
    (c) 6   (d) 9

1. Which image is the most clear and why?

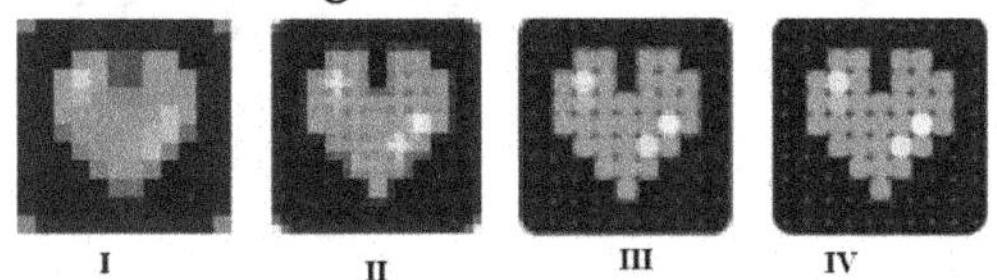

(a) IV, because we can count the dots properly

(b) III and IV as we can identify the colours properly

(c) IV as it has the highest pixels

(d) IV because of the colour contrast

2. Michael pasted her son's picture on a paint file.

Describe what did she do?

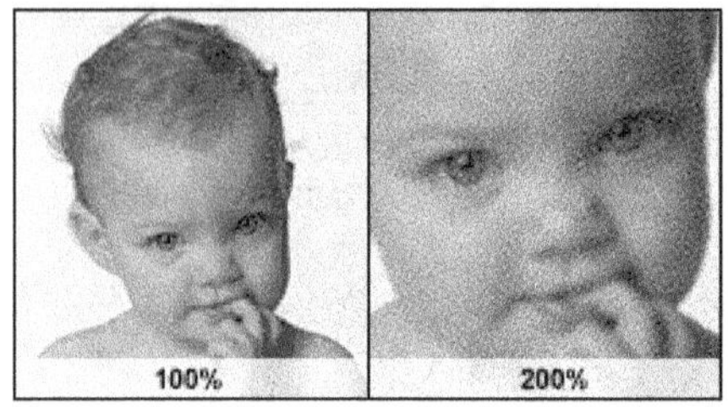

(a) She pasted two images.

(b) She pasted an image and then zoomed it.

(c) She copied the first image and then zoomed it.

(d) She pasted two different images.

Look at the following MS Paint window and answer questions 3–5.

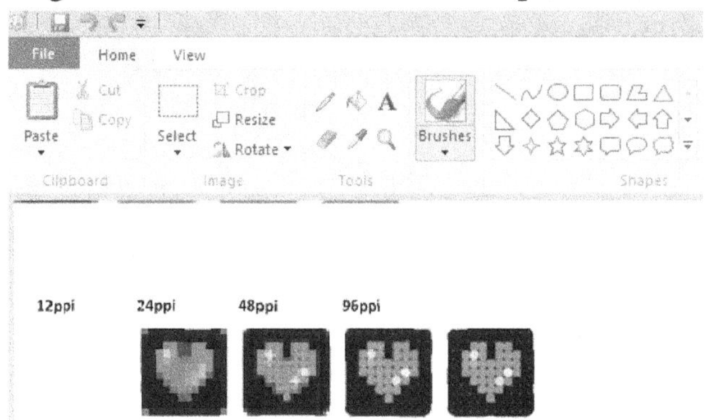

3. If you want to remove the numbers in the picture. What will you use?

(a) 

(b) 

(c) 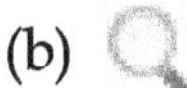
Select

(d) 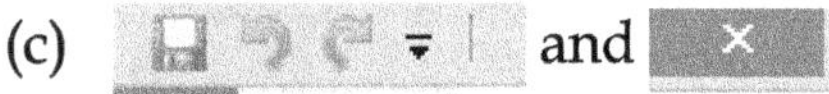

4. If you want to close the MS Paint window, which button will you use?

(a) [×]

(b) [disk/undo/redo toolbar]

(c) [disk/undo/redo toolbar] and [×]

(d) Home   View

5. In the above MS Paint window, you are supposed to enclose the image into an enclosure and fill it with various colours. How many tools will you use?

(a) 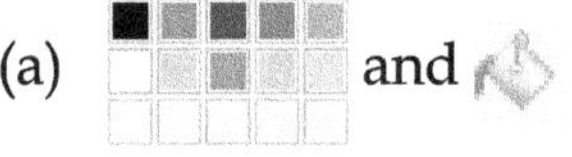 and [fill]

(b) 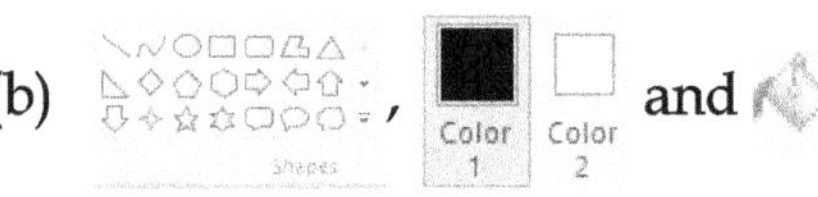 and [fill]

(c) 

(d) 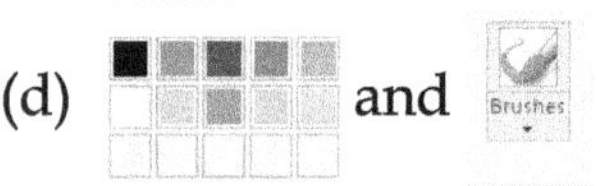 and [Brushes]

1. Choose the correct answers from the hints given and write in front of the picture.

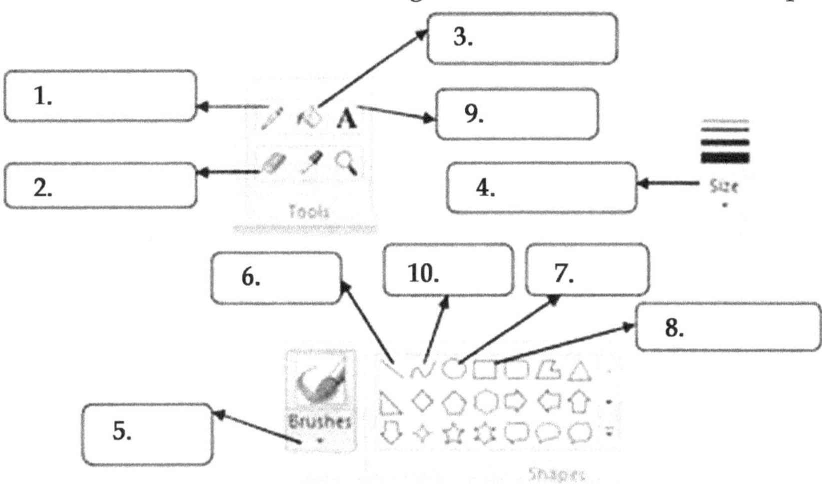

1. Fill with color tool   2. Pencil tool   3. Oval tool   4. Eraser tool   5. Size tool

6. Line tool   7. Rectangle tool   8. Brush tool   9. Curve tool   10. Text tool

Ans.

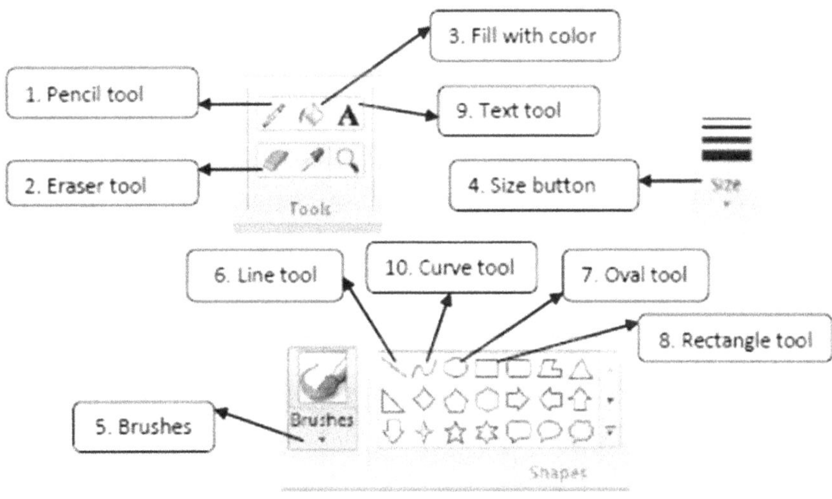

2. What are the options available in the Clipboard Menu?

Ans.

In the MS Paint program, the clipboard menu has three option – Cut, Copy and Paste. These are used to cut the part of an image, copy a part or whole of the image and paste it at the desired location.

3. Write about Crop option.

Ans.

The top button, a diamond shape with a line icon through it is called as Crop. This option is used for erasing or cropping the picture/image without disturbing the selected area/part of the picture. After cropping the large/full picture into the selected area, and after saving it, then the full picture or image before the cropping will not get saved but the image/picture after the cropping with new selected area will be saved.

4. Write the name of tools available in Tools Menu.

Ans.

Pencil, Fill with color, Text tool, Eraser, Color Picker, and the Magnifier are the names of the tools that are available in the Tools Menu.

5. What is Size Tool?

Ans.

This tool is used only when any brush or shape is inserted into the paint program. You will be able to see the small down arrow that is appearing under the Size Tool when any of the shape or brush is been selected (for selecting the line thickness). The line thickness also depends on the brushes that is been chosen.

Latest Developments in IT 8

CHAPTER SUMMARY

IT stands for Information Technology. Information means transfer of knowledge or some message. Technology means Science. Computer and Information Technology involves transfer of message or knowledge through technology. Involvement of IT in daily life is immense and inevitable nowadays. We cannot think of a day without computers/IT. The newspaper that reaches us in the morning involves application of IT in its generation.

Let us discuss some of the latest trendsetters in the field of IT that has changed the modern day life.

Mobile Applications

The cell phones that we use have certainly come a long way since the first wireless models that hit the stores in the 1980s. The earliest mobiles were big in size with small screens and big keypads. Slowly, the size of the phones reduced. But as we entered the 21st century, the mobile screen size increased and the functions became more interactive. The mobiles connected with the internet and became global.

The mobile phones with features other than just calling and SMS are called **Smartphones**. They perform a variety of computing tasks. These mobiles are as good as computers as they have good memory storage and come loaded with lots of applications. The tasks that we perform on our PC today can also be performed on our mobile phone.

The Smartphones today have a specified operating system that has several applications loaded on them. These applications enable us to use the mobile as a device to connect with people across the world and gain immense knowledge.

The three major operating systems are:

1. Windows
2. Android
3. iOS

These three operating systems have certain interesting applications. For example:

Windows Phone

Windows Phone (WP) is a discontinued family of mobile operating systems developed by Microsoft for smartphones as the replacement successor to Windows Mobile and Zune. Windows Phone featured a new user interface derived from the Metro design language. Unlike Windows Mobile, it was primarily aimed at the consumer market rather than the enterprise market. It was first launched in October 2010 with Windows Phone 7. With the diminishing interest and application development for the platform, Microsoft discontinued active development of Windows 10 Mobile in 2017, and the platform was declared end of life on January 14, 2020.

Example of Windows 8.1 screen

2. Android phones are one of the most popular ranges of smartphones. The operating system Android keeps on updating periodically. It is developed by Google. The earliest version of Android was named: Android 1.6 – Donut version. Then came Android 2.0 – Éclair. The latest Android version is Android 13.

Each Android phone has a Google play store that has 'n' number of applications that can be downloaded making phone usage more interesting.

Some of the common Android apps and games are:

3. The third popular OS is iOS. This particular OS is specific to mobile phones developed by a US company Apple.Inc. The devices that have iOS have a small letter 'i' as a prefix, for example: iPad and iPhone.

Some of the common iOS apps are: iBooks, iTunes, iPhoto, etc.

Some common apps on all OS:

 **Twitter:** A Social Networking app.

 **Facebook:** A Social Networking app.

 **Instagram:** A common Picture sharing app.

Some common games on all OS:

Hill Climb Racing

Angry Birds

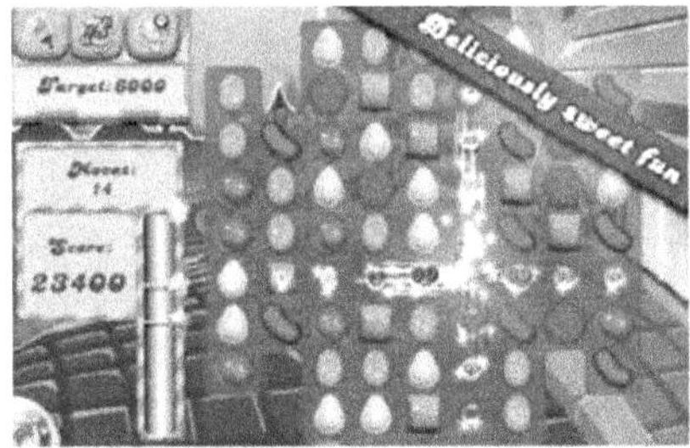

Candy Crush Saga

Technology was used to create Covid Vaccines.

Advanced Computer Applications

There are some very interesting computer applications seen in the present world. Some of them are Drone cameras or flying cameras and e-Book readers.

- **Drone camera:** They are flying cameras which are operated by a remote control device. They help in taking pictures of difficult locations or making videos of a running game. For example: In the game of cricket, Drone cameras help the umpires to decide whether a player is OUT or NOT OUT, in case of a tricky situation. These cameras have many other advanced applications, too.

Example: Remote-controlled Flying Quadcopter: Amazing footage streamed and recorded directly to your smartphone using the inbuilt camera.

- **e-Book Reader:** An e-Book reader is a mobile electronic device that is designed primarily for the purpose of reading digital e-books and periodicals. The major manufacturers of eBook readers are: Amazon's Kindle, Barnes and Noble's NOOK and Apple's iPad. But now, various Android and Windows apps are also available which provide the eBook reading feature, for example: Flipkart eBooks, Google Playbooks, etc.

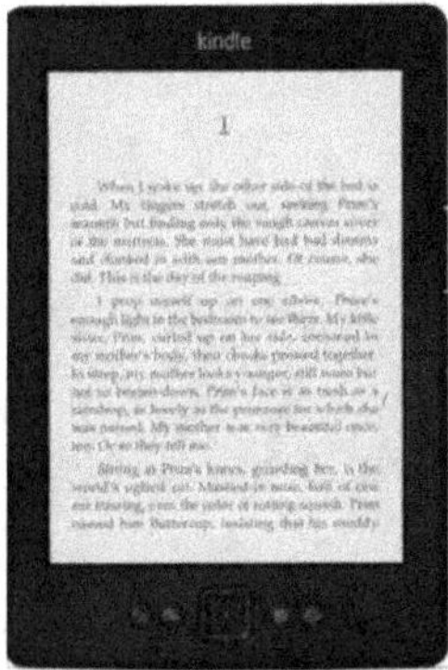

- The mobile phones with features other than just calling and SMS are called Smartphones.
- Android phones are one of the most popular ranges of smartphones.
- Drone camera are flying cameras which are operated by a remote control device.

1. Identify the icon: It is a/an ….

   (a) iOS (b) OS
   (c) Game (d) Social App

2. Mobile app is a kind of
   (a) Game (b) Social network
   (c) Software (d) Mailing app

3. This is not a mobile app
   (a) iOS (b) MS Paint
   (c) Temple Run (d) Instagram

4. IT is used in
   (a) Medical sector
   (b) Army sector
   (c) Education sector
   (d) All the above

5. The following card involves computers for its operation
   (a) A Birthday Card
   (b) A Christmas Card
   (c) A Visiting Card
   (d) A Credit Card

6. The following icon belongs to

   (a) Lumia (b) Samsung
   (c) Apple (d) Blackberry

Directions (7-10): Identify the following images.

7.

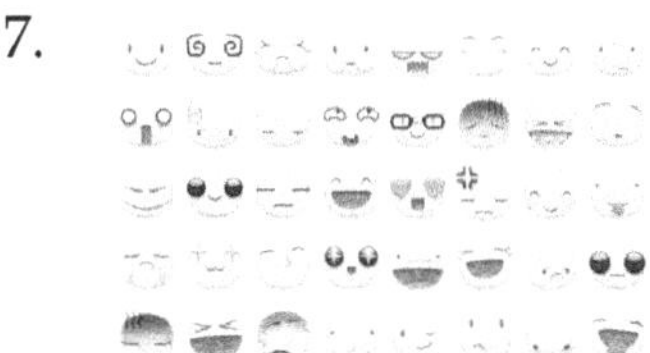

   (a) Smileys (b) App
   (c) Game (d) OS

8.

   (a) Software
   (b) OS
   (c) Gaming software
   (d) iOS

9.

   (a) Social networking site with an e-Book reader advertisement
   (b) e-Book reader advertisement
   (c) Social networking site
   (d) Android app

10.

   (a) Flying robot
   (b) Flying camera
   (c) Toy helicopter
   (d) Remote controlled toy

11. Through this we connect to the internet
    (a) 3G
    (b) Telephone
    (c) WiFi and 3G
    (d) Television

12. This is the smallest smart device.
    (a) iPad (b) iPhone
    (c) Tablet (d) Laptop

13. 

Who will help the umpire take the decision?
(a) The bowler   (b) The audience
(c) A Drone   (d) A computer

14. Which is the best suited definition for a smartphone?
(a) A big-screen phone
(b) A mobile phone that performs many of the functions of a computer
(c) A phone with touchscreen
(d) A phone with lots of games

15. 

What are the children wearing?
(a) A magical gadget
(b) A 3-D glass
(c) A sun glass
(d) A toy

16. Android is developed by
(a) Microsoft   (b) Adobe
(c) Mozilla   (d) Google

17. Which OS has its versions named based on various sugary products?
(a) Android   (b) Windows
(c) Adobe   (d) Mac

18. Which is the latest version of Android?
(a) KitKat
(b) Lollipop
(c) Gingerbread
(d) None of these

19. This is an anti-virus program.
(a) McAfee
(b) MS Paint
(c) Hill Climber
(d) Candy Crush

20. Where can you insert this kind of object?

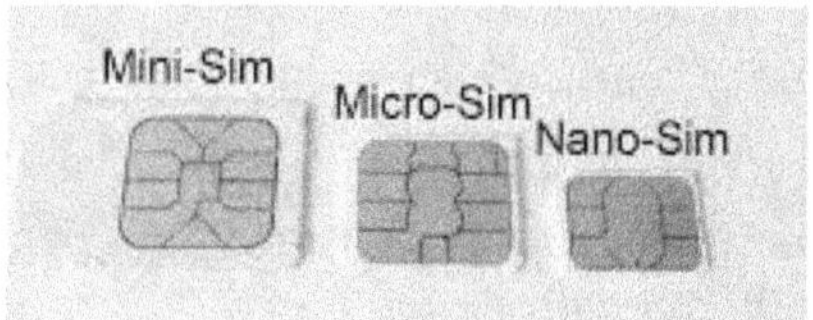

(a) Computer
(b) Mobile
(c) Mobile and computer
(d) Mobile and tablet

1. The following device is specialised for

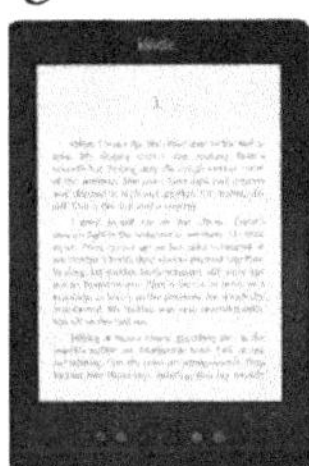

   (a) Reading books
   (b) It is an electronic library for reading books.
   (c) It is a document creator.
   (d) It is an iPad.

2. Which device is the latest invention?

   (a) 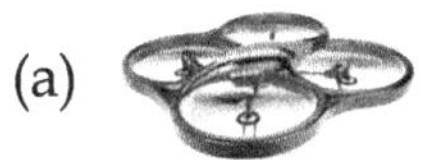   (b) 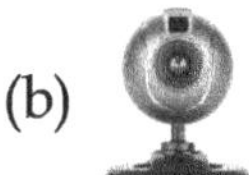

   (c)    (d) 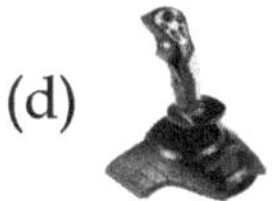

3. The given device can be read by __________.

   (a) Smartphones
   (b) Tablets
   (c) Calculators
   (d) Both (a) and (b)

4. This is an image of which operating system version on Android?

   (a) Lollipop   (b) Jellybean
   (c) Kitkat   (d) Cupcake

5. This is an image of which operating system version on Android?

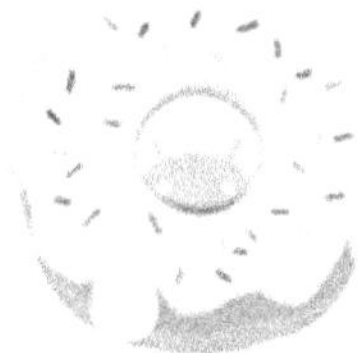

   (a) Donut   (b) Lollipop
   (c) Cupcake   (d) Honeycomb

SECTION 2
LOGICAL REASONING

Patterns

1

Learning Objectives : In this chapter, students will learn about:
- ✓ Finding the missing number in a series
- ✓ Finding the missing part in a figure

CHAPTER SUMMARY

Pattern is a repeated sequence of letters, numbers and shapes, which has a particular logical design. Patterns can be classified as follows.

1. Identification of the missing number in the number series or missing letters in the letter series pattern.

Example: 10, 22, 34, ____, 58……

Sol.

The pattern followed in the above example is addition of 12 in each number to get the next number.

Hence the missing number will be 46.

2. Identification of missing part in a figure.

Example:

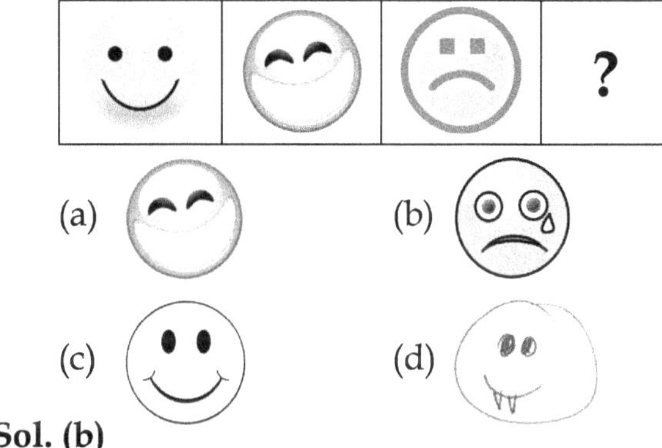

Sol. (b)

In the above series, smileys follow normal to extreme facial expressions.

1. Find the missing number in the given number pattern, if the series in both the patterns follows the same rule.

Pattern-I	Pattern-II
22	60
30	68
38	?

(a) 76   (b) 66
(c) 36   (d) 56

2. Find the missing number in the given number pattern.

80, 70, 55, 45, ?

(a) 25   (b) 30
(c) 20   (d) 35

3. Complete the pattern by choosing the next figure.

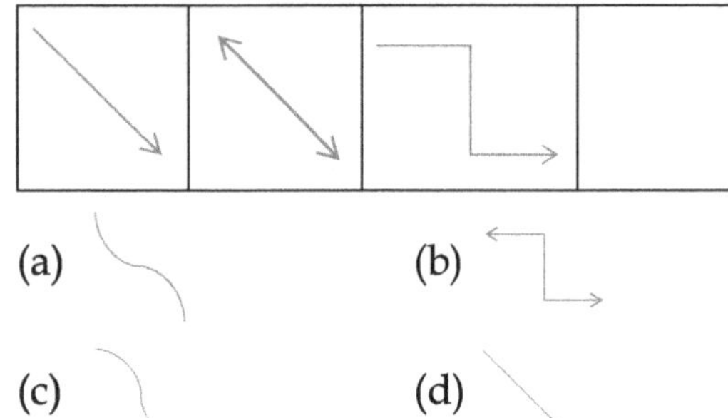

(a)   (b)

(c)   (d)

4. Complete the pattern by choosing the next figure.

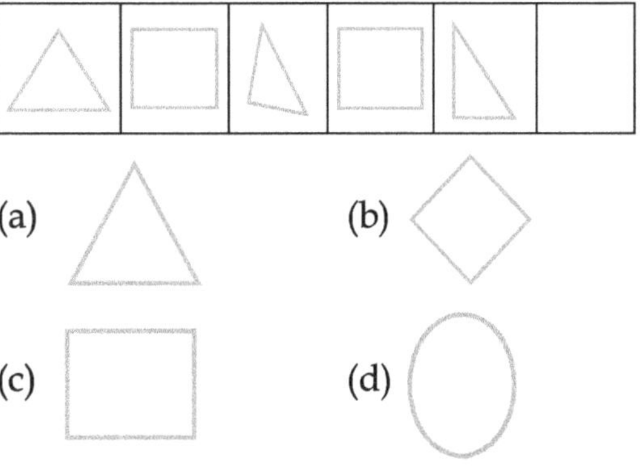

(a)   (b)

(c)   (d)

5. Complete the pattern by choosing the next figure.

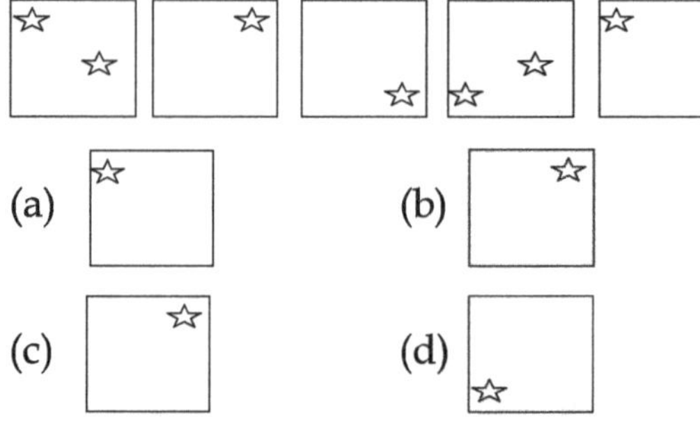

(a)   (b)

(c)   (d)

6. Find the missing number in the given number pattern.

428, 418, 430, ?, 432, 422, 434, ?

(a) 418, 436   (b) 422, 444
(c) 420, 446   (d) 420, 424

7. Which of the following replaces the question mark (?) in given number patterns?

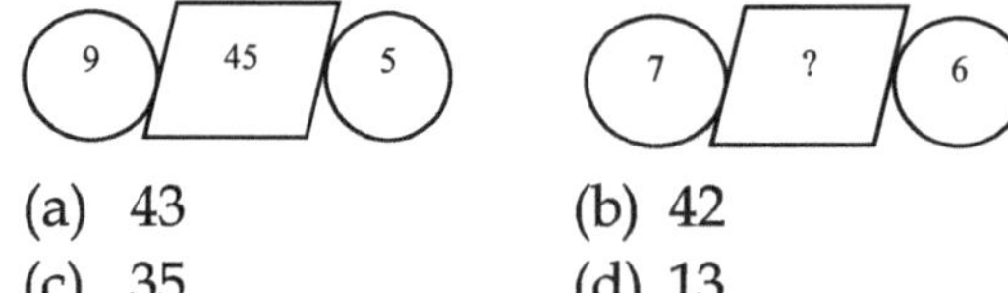

(a) 43   (b) 42
(c) 35   (d) 13

8. Complete the number pattern given below.

4, 12, 36, ?, 324, 972

(a) 72   (b) 216
(c) 112   (d) 108

9. Complete the pattern by choosing the next figure.

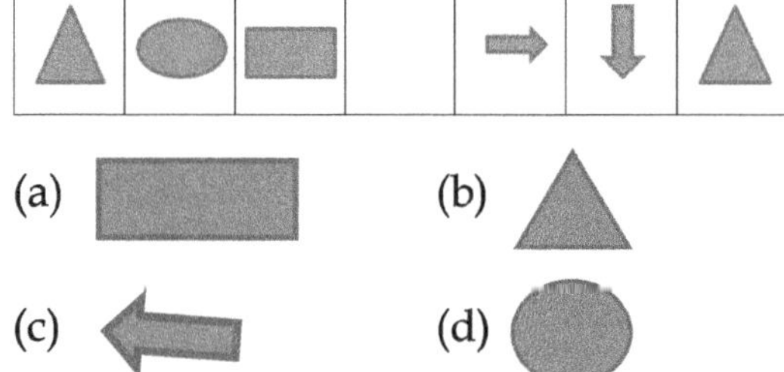

(a)   (b)

(c)   (d)

10. Complete the pattern by choosing the next figure.

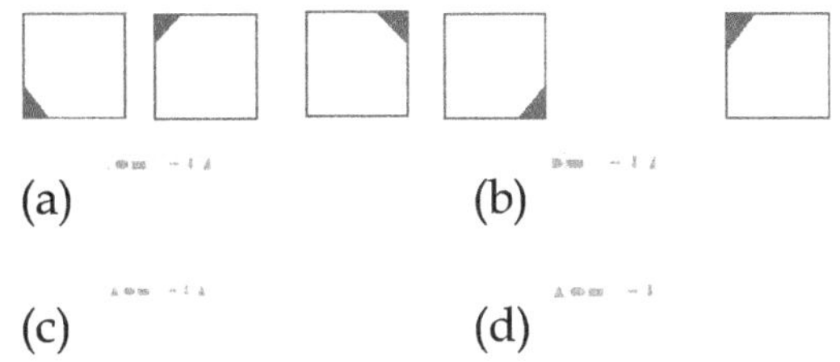

(a)   (b)

(c)   (d)

11. Complete the pattern by choosing the next figure.

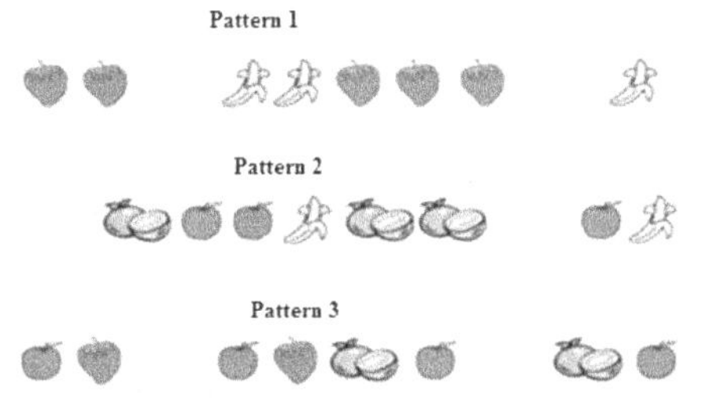

(a) Pattern 1:   ,   ; Pattern 2:   ,
     Pattern 3:   ,

(b) Pattern 1:   ,   ; Pattern 2:   ;
     Pattern 3:   ,

(c) Pattern 1:   ,   ; Pattern 2:
     Pattern 3:   ,

(d) Pattern 1:   ,   ; Pattern 2:   ,
     Pattern 3:   ,

12. What comes next in the alphabetical pattern?

ACF, IKN, PRU, TVY, ?

(a) ABE   (b) RQT
(c) RTW   (d) RTV

13. Complete the pattern by choosing the next figure.

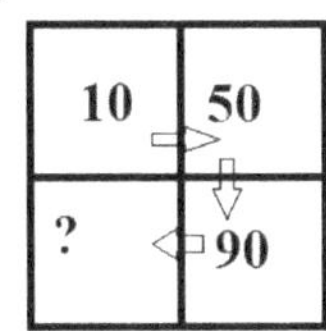

(a) 120   (b) 130
(c) 140   (d) 150

14. Which of the following replaces the question mark (?) in given number patterns?

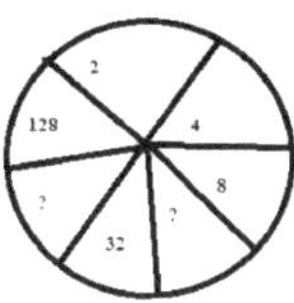

(a) 24, 16   (b) 16, 64
(c) 44, 64   (d) 64, 24

15. What comes next in the alphabetical pattern?

J K L D K L J K L D K L J K L D K L J ?

(a) D   (b) L
(c) K   (d) J

16. How many ants will be there in pattern 3?

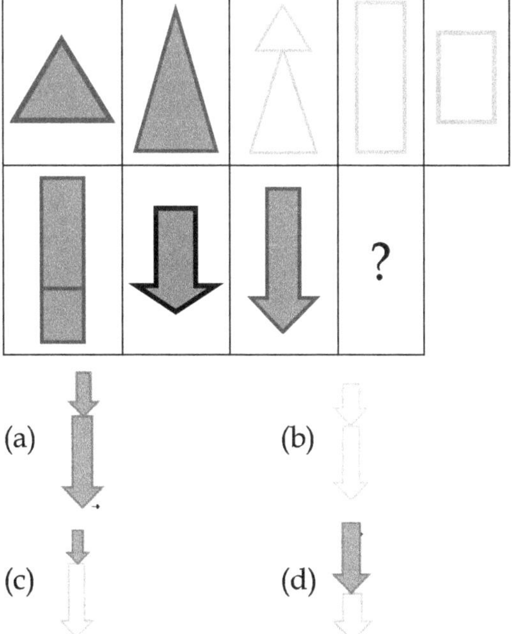

(a) 4   (b) 6
(c) 8   (d) 5

17. Which of the following replaces the question mark (?) in given pattern?

(a)   (b)

(c)   (d)

18. Which of the following replaces the question mark (?) in given number patterns?

(a) 357 (b) 362
(c) 338 (d) 346

19. Look at the given pattern.

How would you show this pattern using letters?

(a) AAVVAAA (b) TTTVTTT
(c) VVTTTVV (d) VTTTVTTT

20. Which of the following replaces the question mark (?) in given number patterns?

A = 1, B = 2, C = 3, D = 4...

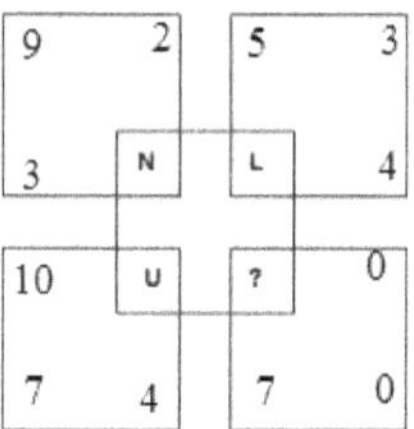

9	2	5	3
3	N	L	4
10	U	?	0
7	4	7	0

(a) H (b) L
(c) J (d) G

National Cyber Olympiad – 2

Odd One Out   2

Learning Objectives : In this chapter, students will learn about:
- ✓ Odd One Out

CHAPTER SUMMARY

Odd one out is pointing out that component which does not fit in a group. For example, a bird among a group of animals is the odd one.

In these types of questions, we need to identify the odd object or subject among various options.

Example 1: Choose the odd one out.

- (a) Cooler
- (b) Fan
- (c) Air conditioner
- (d) Water heater

Sol. (d)

Among all the options, option D, water heater is the odd one out, as all the other options provide cooling while water heater is used for heating.

Example 2: There are four figures given below. Choose the odd one out.

(a)   (b)

(c)   (d)

Sol. (c)

Option C is the odd one out here. All the shapes except the circle have corners.

1. Choose the odd one out.

   (a) 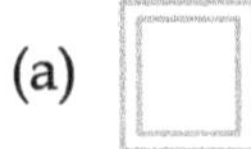 (b) 

   (c)  (d) 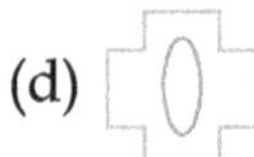

2. Choose the odd one out.
   16, 20, 24, 28, 32, 38, 40
   (a) 20 (b) 28
   (c) 33 (d) 38

3. Choose the odd one out.

   (a)  (b) 

   (c)  (d) 

4. Choose the odd one out.

   (a)  (b) 

   (c)  (d) 

5. Choose the odd one out.

   (a)  (b) 

   (c)  (d) 

6. Choose the odd one out.

   (a) 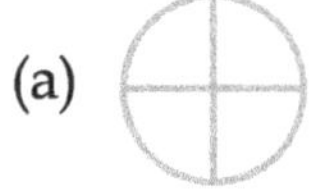 (b) 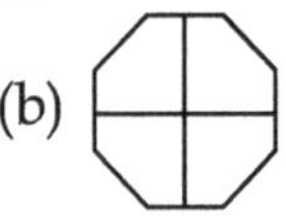

   (c)  (d)

7. Look at the following pictures carefully and choose the odd one out.

   (a)  (b) 

   (c)  (d) 

8. Choose the odd one out.

   (a) 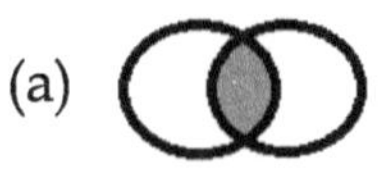 (b) 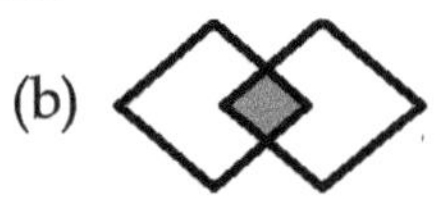

   (c)  (d) 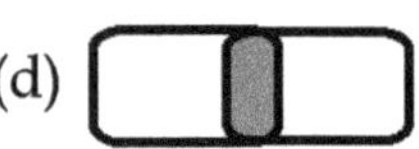

9. Choose the odd one out.
   72, 36, 18, 6, 4.5
   (a) 4.5 (b) 6
   (c) 3 (d) 18

10. Choose the odd one out.

    (a)  (b) 

    (c)  (d) 

11. Choose the odd one out.

    (a) 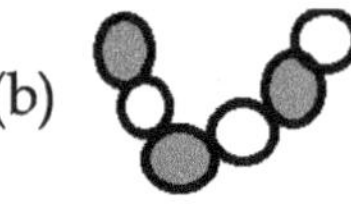 (b) 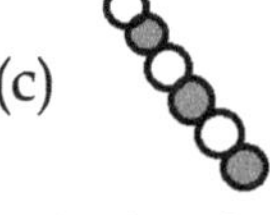

    (c)  (d) 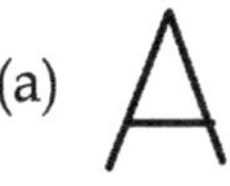

12. Which of the following alphabet is the odd one on the basis of geometrical lines?

    (a) A (b) O

    (c) E (d) W

13. Choose the odd one out.
    (a) Eye (b) Radar
    (c) Level (d) Money

14. Choose the odd one out.

    (a) 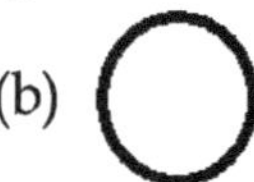 (b) 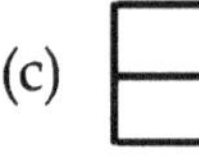

    (c)  (d) 

15. Choose the odd one out.

(a) 
(b) 
(c) 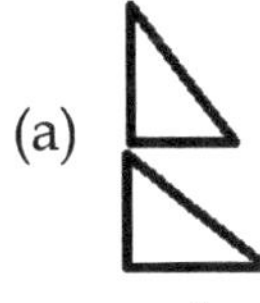
(d) 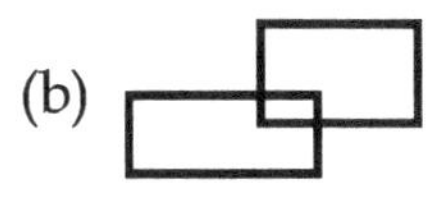

16. Choose the odd one out.

(a) 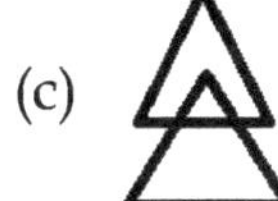
(b) 
(c)
(d)

17. Choose the odd one out.
   (a) E   (b) O
   (c) A   (d) T

18. Choose the odd one out.
   (a) Candy Crush Saga
   (b) Tennis
   (c) Temple Run
   (d) Subway Surfers

19. Choose the odd one out.
   (a) Knee   (b) Arm
   (c) Hand   (d) Fingers

20. Choose the odd one out.
   (a) Belt   (b) Scarf
   (c) Capris   (d) Necklace

Series Completion 3

CHAPTER SUMMARY

Series completion is a sequential arrangement of numbers or letters which follow a certain and definite pattern.

Type 1: Number Series

In number series, a series of numbers is provided with one or more than one missing numbers which follow a certain pattern using different fundamentals, like subtraction, addition, multiplication and division.

Example 1: Look at the series below and find the missing number.

10, 25, 40, 55, ?

(a) 75   (b) 70

(c) 65   (d) 85

Sol. (b)

Add 15 in each number.

Example 2: Look at the series below and find the missing number.

8, 14, 26, 50, ?

(a) 98   (b) 96

(c) 100   (d) 102

Sol. (a)

Firstly, a number is multiplied by 2 and then 2 is subtracted to get the next number in the series:

$$8 \rightarrow 8 \times 2 = 16 - 2 = 14.$$

Type 2: Letter Series

In letter series, a series of letters is provided with one or more than one missing letters which follows a certain pattern.

Example 1: Find the next term in the series.

C, F, I, L, ?

(a) N   (b) O

(c) P   (d) Q

Sol. (b)

Each next letter of the series is the next third letter of the previous letter:

$$C \rightarrow D \ (1), E \ (2) \text{ and } \rightarrow F \ (3)$$

1. Find the next number in the series.
   40, 30, 22, 16, ?
   (a) 14   (B 12
   (c) 10   (d) 18

2. Find the next number in the series.
   1, 3, 9, 27, 81, ?
   (a) 243   (b) 253
   (c) 250   (d) 216

3. Find the next number in the series.
   2, 4, 12, 24, 72, 144, ?
   (a) 288   (b) 382
   (c) 432   (d) 576

4. Find the next number in the series.
   108, 54, 18, 9, ?
   (a) 3   (b) 6
   (c) 2   (d) 18

5. Find the next number in the series.
   3, 4, 7, 12, 19, ?
   (a) 26   (b) 27
   (c) 30   (d) 28

6. Find the next letter in the series.
   A, D, G, J, ?
   (a) K   (b) N
   (c) M   (d) P

7. What should come next in the following letter series?
   E F G H I J E F G H I E F G H
   (a) G H F   (b) J H I
   (c) E F G   (d) F G H

8. What should come next in the following letter series?
   C, H, M, R, ?
   (a) X   (b) W
   (c) U   (d) V

9. What should come next in the following letter series?
   RS, PQ, NO, MN, ?
   (a) LM   (b) JK
   (c) KL   (d) OP

10. How many V's are there in the given series?
    AAVAAVVWWVWWVVMMMMVPV
    PPSVSSVTT
    (a) 8   (b) 9
    (c) 10   (d) 11

11. What should come next in the series?
    MNOP, NOPM, OPMN, ?, MNOP
    (a) PMNO   (b) OPMN
    (c) MNOP   (d) NMOP

12. Find the next number in the series.
    5, 25, 125, 625, ?
    (a) 1250   (b) 3125
    (c) 15625   (d) 925

13. In the given series, take a look at the letter pattern and then fill the blank.
    DGH, EIJ, FKL, ____, HOP
    (a) GMN   (b) GNM
    (c) MNO   (d) NMI

14. Complete the following series.
    GFE, JIH, MLK, PON, ____, VUT
    (a) SRQ   (b) SQR
    (c) RSQ   (d) RQS

15. What should come next in the series?
    MAT-CAT, GUN-RUN, SAT-
    (a) MPE   (b) STO
    (c) HAT   (d) RDU

16. Complete the following series.
    X, V, S, O, J, ?
    (a) E   (b) F
    (c) C   (d) D

17. Find the missing number in the given series.

    | 18 | 21 | 24 |
    | 28 | 30 | 32 |
    | 15 | 21 | ? |

    (a) 27   (b) 18
    (c) 40   (d) 24

18. Find the next term in the series.

B – 2, D – 4, F– 8, H–16, J–32, ?

(a) M– 48   (b) M– 64

(c) L– 48   (d) L– 64

19. Which letter is moving in the series according to the blanks?

XYZ _XY Y_X XY_

(a) X   (b) XY

(c) Z   (d) YZ

20. Complete the following series.

16, 15, 13, ____, 6, 1

(a) 11   (b) 9

(c) 10   (d) 8

Analogy   4

Learning Objectives : In this chapter, students will learn about:
- ✓ Analogy

CHAPTER SUMMARY

Analogy means a comparison between two things that have some relationship on the basis of their similarities.

In these types of questions, we have to find out that relation among different options.

Example 1: Find out the relation.

    Text: Paper: Paper: ?

    (a) Pen   (b) Book
    (c) Ink   (d) Pencil

Sol. (b)

    As text is found in paper similarly paper is found in book.

Example 2: Find the missing shape by identifying the relationship.

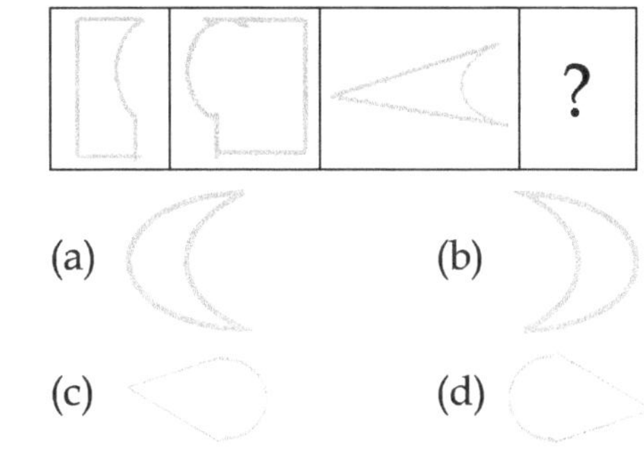

(a)   (b)

(c)   (d)

Sol. (d)

    In the figure, the curved part comes outwards and the pattern is reversed.

1. Find out the relation.

   Pen : Ink : : Pencil : ?
   - (a) Iron
   - (b) Plastic
   - (c) Graphite
   - (d) Carbon

2. Find out the relation.

   Uttarakhand: Dehradun : : Goa: ?
   - (a) Patna
   - (b) Panaji
   - (c) Jaipur
   - (d) Gandhinagar

3. Find the missing shape by identifying the relationship.

   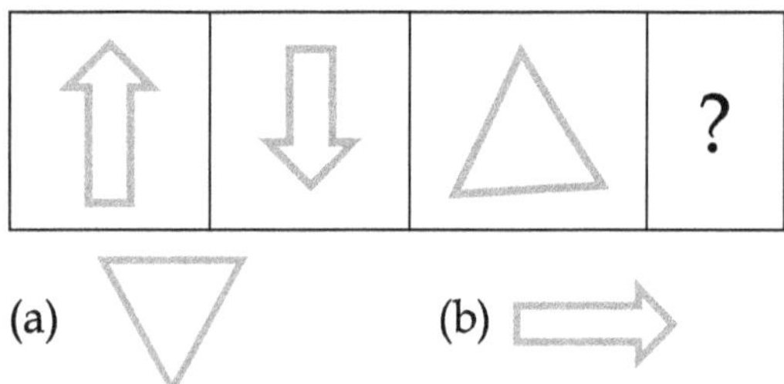

   - (a) 
   - (b) 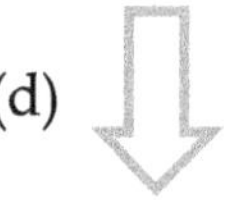
   - (c)
   - (d)

4. Find the missing shape by identifying the relationship.

   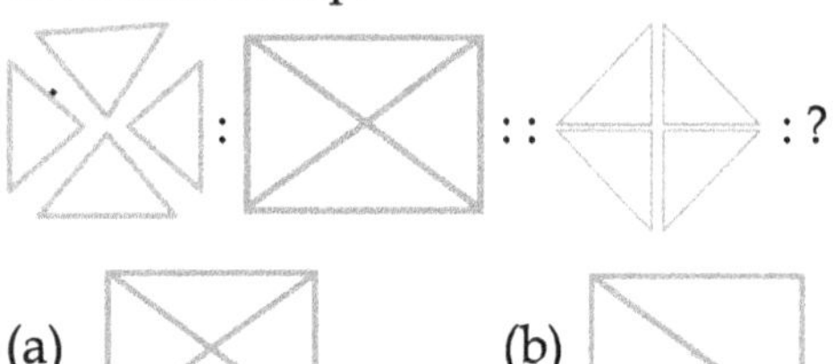

   - (a) 
   - (b) 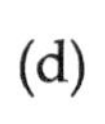
   - (c)
   - (d)

5. Find out the relation.

   Father : Mother : : Grandfather :?
   - (a) Grandson
   - (b) Daughter
   - (c) Grandmother
   - (d) Granddaughter

6. Find out the relation.

   Snake : Turtle : : Lizard :?
   - (a) Cat
   - (b) Fly
   - (c) Dog
   - (d) Crocodile

7. Find the missing shape by identifying the relationship.

   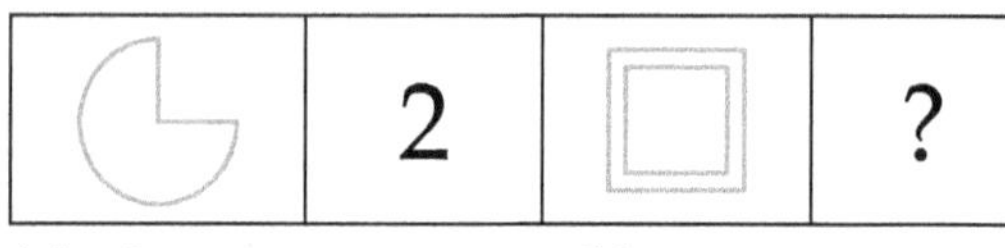

   - (a) 8
   - (b) 4
   - (c) 6
   - (d) 10

8. Find the missing shape by identifying the relationship.

   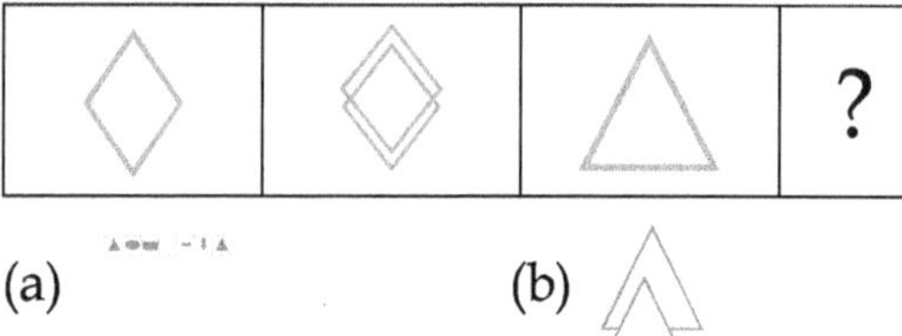

   - (a) 
   - (b)
   - (c)
   - (d)

9. Find the missing shape by identifying the relationship.

   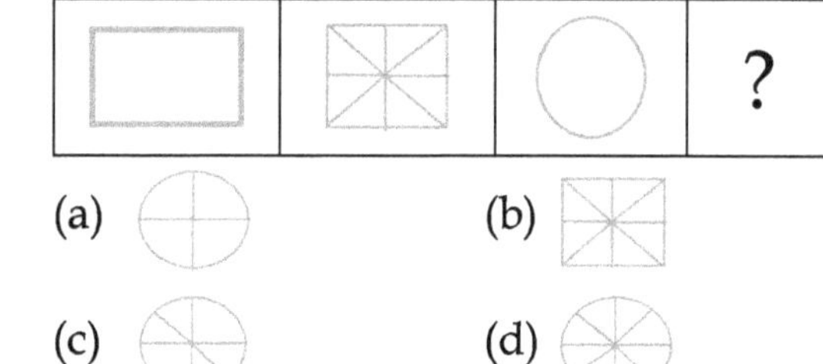

   - (a)
   - (b)
   - (c)
   - (d)

10. Find the missing shape by identifying the relationship.

    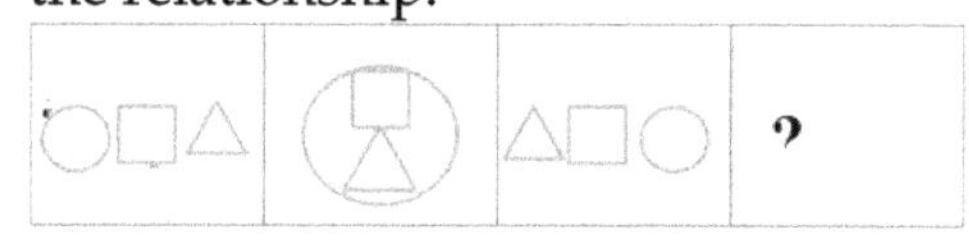

    - (a) 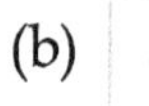
    - (b)
    - (c)
    - (d)

11. Find the missing shape by identifying the relationship.

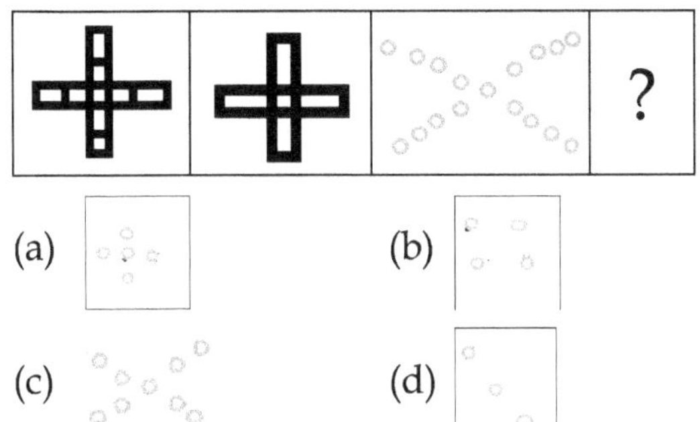

(a)   (b)

(c)   (d)

12. Find the missing shape by identifying the relationship.

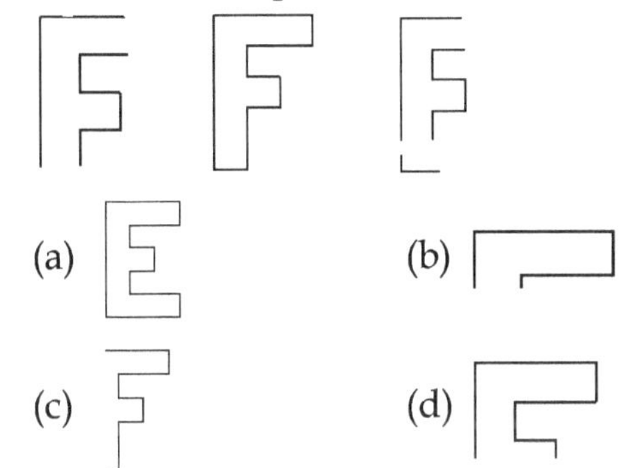

(a)   (b)

(c)   (d)

Choose the word which best completes each analogy for question number 13 to 16.

13. Elbow is to hand as fingers are to
    (a) Feet   (b) Palm
    (c) Leg   (d) Body

14. A dolphin is to sea as a chicken is to ______.
    (a) Burrow   (b) Stable
    (c) Hive   (d) Coop

15. A week is to 7 days as an hour is to ________ minutes and ________ seconds
    (a) 60 min, 60 sec
    (b) 100 min, 3600 sec
    (c) 60 min, 3600 sec
    (d) 3600 min, 60 sec

16. Bark is to tree as skin is to:
    (a) Fur   (b) Human body
    (c) Plastic   (d) Vegetables

17. Find the missing shape by identifying the relationship.

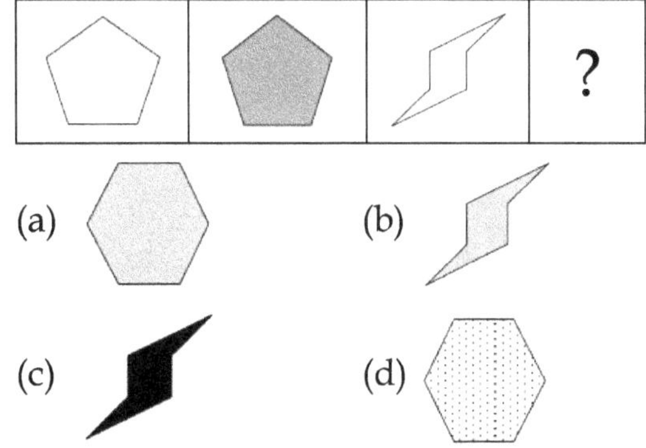

(a)   (b)

(c)   (d)

18. Find the missing shape by identifying the relationship.

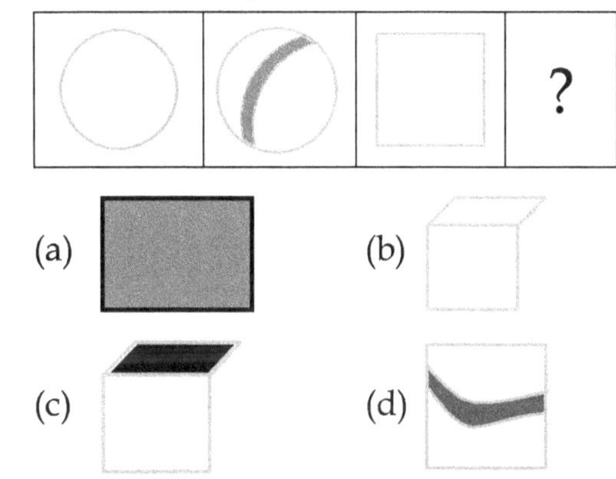

(a)   (b)

(c)   (d)

19. Find the missing shape by identifying the relationship.

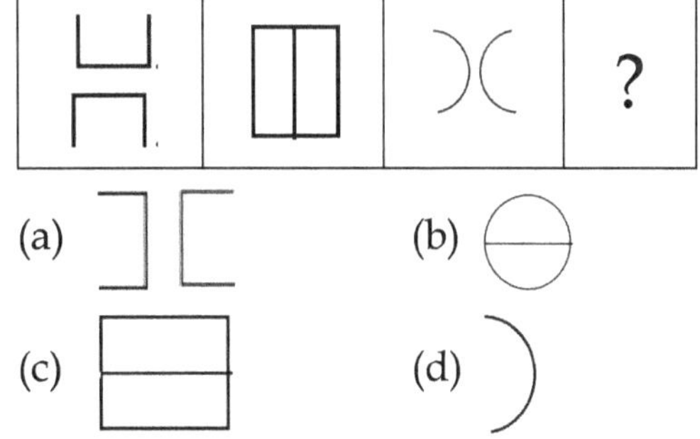

(a)   (b)

(c)   (d)

20. Find the missing shape by identifying the relationship:
    Guitar: Music, Food:
    (a) Energy   (b) Run
    (c) Jump   (d) Rest

Coding and Decoding   5

 **Learning Objectives :** In this chapter, students will learn about:
- ✓ Letter to letter
- ✓ Letter to number
- ✓ Miscellaneous types

CHAPTER SUMMARY

Coding-decoding is a signal system which is used in conveying the messages by using certain codes to represent letters or numbers. It is a web of symbols, letters or words.

For example, If a glass is coded as "drink", it will be called as a drink only.

There are three main types of coding-decoding categories. They are

(a) Letter to letter

(b) Letter to number

(c) Miscellaneous types

Example 1: If GIVE is written as EVIG, OVER is written as REVO, then how will 'DISK' be written in that same code?

   (a) SIDK   (b) KISD

   (c) KIDS   (d) KSID

Sol. (d)

Reverse the alphabet.

1. G = 4. E	1. O = 4. R	1. D = 4. K
2. I = 3. V	2. V = 3. E	2. I = 3. S
3. V = 2. I	3. E = 2. V	3. S = 2. I
4. E = 1. G	4. R = 1. O	4. K = 1. D

Example 2: If BAT is coded as 23, then EAGLE is coded as ____________.

   (a) 26   (b) 30

   (c) 36   (d) 20

Sol. (b)

Hint: As A = 1, B = 2, C = 3 and so on, then,

B A T = 1 + 2 + 20 = 23

Similarly,

E A G L E + 5 + 1 + 7 + 12 + 5 = 30

Example 3: A curtain has three colours: red, white and black, If red is called white, white is called black, black is called green. Then which colour is on the last strip of the curtain?

   (a) Green   (b) Black

   (c) Red   (d) White

Sol. (a)

Last strip on the curtain is of black colour and black is called green.

Directions (1–3):

Alphabet in natural series are:

A = 1	B = 2	C = 3	D = 4	E = 5	F = 6
G = 7	H = 8	I = 9	J = 10	K = 11	L = 12
M = 13	N = 14	O = 15	P = 16	Q = 17	R = 18
S = 19	T = 20	U = 21	V = 22	W = 23	X = 24
Y = 25	Z = 26				

1. If TABLE is written as 40, then CHAIR will be written as ______.
   - (a) 39
   - (b) 38
   - (c) 26
   - (d) 36

2. If CARROT = 75, then RADISH will be written as ______.
   - (a) 76
   - (b) 36
   - (c) 59
   - (d) 85

3. If SEA = 13, then YAK will be written as ______.
   - (a) 16
   - (b) 13
   - (c) 17
   - (d) 8

4. If HELP is coded as 8-5-12-16, then how will you code HORSE?
   - (a) 8-18-19-15-5
   - (b) 8-15-5-19-18
   - (c) 8-15-18-19-5
   - (d) 8-19-15-5-18

5. If GOAT is coded as 7-15-1-20, then how will you code SHEEP?
   - (a) 19-13-5-5-16
   - (b) 19-8-5-5-16
   - (c) 19-15-5-5-8
   - (d) 19-8-5-5-16

6. If house is called nest, nest is called hole, hole is called den, then in which place do birds live?
   - (a) Den
   - (b) Hole
   - (c) Nest
   - (d) House

7. If grass is called insects, insects are called birds, birds are called owl, then what is the name of the insects?
   - (a) Grass
   - (b) Insects
   - (c) Owl
   - (d) Birds

8. If tiger is called lion, lion is called elephant, elephant is called bear, then who is the king of jungle?
   - (a) Tiger
   - (b) Lion
   - (c) Bear
   - (d) Elephant

Directions (9–10): If night is called evening, evening is called day, day is called morning, morning is called night, then answer the following questions:

9. What is the time for sunset?
   - (a) Day
   - (b) Morning
   - (c) Evening
   - (d) Night

10. When do we wake up?
    - (a) Morning
    - (b) Day
    - (c) Evening
    - (d) Night

11. If January is called February, February is called March, March is called April, April is called January, then which of these is called fourth month of the Year?
    - (a) February
    - (b) April
    - (c) January
    - (d) March

12. If Sun is called Moon, Moon is called Earth, Earth is called Mars, Mars is called Sun, then we live on ______.
    - (a) Mars
    - (b) Earth
    - (c) Moon
    - (d) Sun

13. If ◇ can be written as 4, ○ can be written as 0, △ can be written as 3, ⬡ can be written as ______.
    - (a) 4
    - (b) 6
    - (c) 5
    - (d) 3

14. In a certain code, HORSE is written as PMNBY and CAMEL is written as LOQYK. How will HARE be written in that same code?
    - (a) PONY
    - (b) PLOY
    - (c) OPNY
    - (d) NYOP

15. In a certain code language, CAT is written as XZG. How will TEA be written in that same code language?
    - (a) VZG
    - (b) ZGV
    - (c) GVZ
    - (d) GZV

16. In a certain code language, DOLL is written as WLOO. How will TEDDY be written in that same code?
   (a) GVWVB
   (b) WGBVW
   (c) GVWWB
   (d) GWWVB

17. If MIRROR is coded as RORRIM, then CAMERA will be coded as?
   (a) AREMAC
   (b) ARECAM
   (c) AREMCA
   (d) AREAMC

18. If DOORMAT is coded as TAMROOD, then REFRIGERATOR will be coded as ______.
   (a) ROTAREGERFRI
   (b) ROTAREGIRFER
   (c) ROTAREGIRRFE
   (d) ROTAREGIRFRE

19. If '853' is coded '631', '974' is coded '752', then '594' is coded as ______.
   (a) 327   (b) 632
   (c) 532   (d) 372

20. If '2961' is coded '1850, '3854' is coded '2743, then '1539' is coded as ______.
   (a) 4860   (b) 0428
   (c) 4806   (d) 0529

Ranking Test 6

Learning Objectives : In this chapter, students will learn about:
- ✓ Ranking Test

CHAPTER SUMMARY

Ranking is based on the arrangement of different things like, persons, objects or characters based on some special feature in a specific order.

Ranking test can be of various categories:

1. In the first category, position or rank of an object or a person is identified from left end or right end or from top or bottom.

2. Second category is based on interchanging the positions of two persons or objects.

3. Third category is based on the position of any person or object with respect to the other person or object.

4. Fourth category is based on the identification of position or object after removing some of the objects in the series.

Example 1: Observe the following figures carefully.

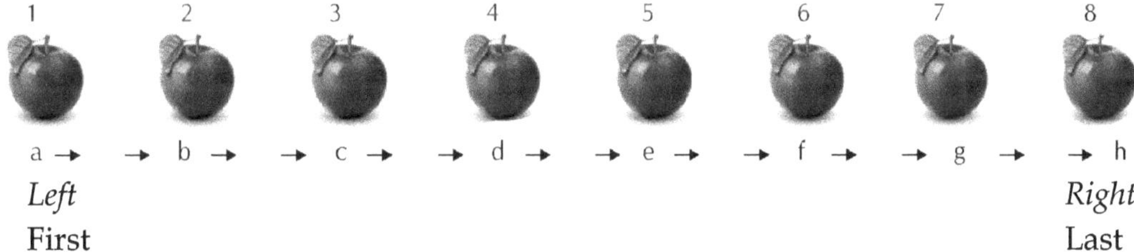

Apple at the fourth position is at the immediate left of the ______ apple.

   (a) c   (b) e

   (c) a   (d) f

Sol. (b)

   d number apple is at the 4th position and it is at the immediate left to the e apple.

Example 2: Observe the following figures carefully:

If Summi's position is interchanged with Somya's postion, then which girl will be positioned at 6th position?

(a) Somya (b) Summi
(c) Somi (d) Sonu

Sol. (b)

Example 3: If the apple at the extreme right is eaten by someone, which apple will become the fifth from the right end?

Left | | | | | | | Right

E F O G H P I J

(a) H (b) G
(c) O (d) P

Sol. (c)

Direction (1-5): Observe the given figure carefully and answer the following questions.

Left (first)

P   N   I   K   O   J   M   L

1. Which bird is seventh from the right end?
    (a) M
    (b) L
    (c) N
    (d) P
2. Bird O is second to the right of bird ____.
    (a) P
    (b) I
    (c) M
    (d) N

3. If bird P and I interchange their positions, then bird ______ is at the left end.
    (a) I
    (b) L
    (c) P
    (d) M
4. Bird J is just left to ______ bird.
    (a) N
    (b) O
    (c) M
    (d) L
5. Bird ______ is the sixth bird to the right of bird N.
    (a) J
    (b) K
    (c) M
    (d) L

Directions (6–10): Observe the given figure carefully and answer the following questions.

Left   Right

D   J   E   M   K   F   I   L   G   H

6. Which umbrella is 10th from the right end?
    (a) D
    (b) H
    (c) J
    (d) G
7. If Suhani took the immediate left umbrella of the umbrella K, which umbrella did she take?
    (a) M
    (b) N
    (c) F
    (d) H
8. Which umbrella is fifth from umbrella E towards right?
    (a) L
    (b) H
    (c) G
    (d) M
9. Umbrella E is ________ to the left of umbrella F.
    (a) Second
    (b) Fourth
    (c) Fifth
    (d) Third
10. Umbrella ______ is the right of F and left of L.
    (a) K
    (b) I
    (c) L
    (d) G

Directions (11-13): Observe the given figure carefully and answer the following questions.

Left/First

P   Q   T   V   W   R   U   S

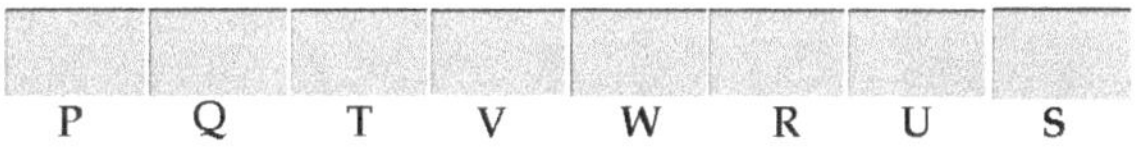

11. W brick is at the 5th position from the left. Now find out the name and position (from the left) of the brick which is at the immediate left of the W brick.
    (a) V, fifth
    (b) R, fifth
    (c) V, fourth
    (d) R, fourth
12. If P brick and U brick interchange their position, then brick ________ is at the left end.
    (a) Q
    (b) U
    (c) P
    (d) S
13. Which brick is seventh to the right of brick P?
    (a) S
    (b) U
    (c) R
    (d) P

14. If a rows of trees are numbered as 1,2,3,4,... till 50, then how many trees will be there between 10th and 38th tree?
    (a) 28 (b) 30
    (c) 27 (d) 20

Directions (15–16): Observe the given figure carefully and answer the following questions.

Left/First

15. Sushma is standing between _______ and _______.
    (a) Reema and Ananya
    (b) Meghna and Reema
    (c) Jyoti and Shiva
    (d) Ananya and Shiva

16. If Ananya and Shiva interchange their positions, then Ananya will be at the immediate left of _______.
    (a) Reema (b) Jyoti
    (c) Meghna (d) Sushma

17. There are 20 students in a class. Six of them are standing, and 10 of them are sitting in the class. Now find out the number of remaining students in the class.
    (a) 16 (b) 4
    (c) 6 (d) 8

Directions (18–20): There are 10 rows of students in a class, five students in each row. Rohit is sitting at the 3rd position (from the left) of the fourth row, Sumit is at the 5th position in the same row, and Sneha at the immediate right of Rohit.

18. Where is Sneha sitting?
    (a) 6th (b) 10th
    (c) 4th (d) 5th

19. On which row, from the back, is Rohit sitting?
    (a) 4th (b) 7th
    (c) 6th (d) 5th

20. If Rohit is sitting at the 8th position from the front, then what will be his position from the end of the row among 20 students?
    (a) 32rd (b) 13th
    (c) 34th (d) 20th

Embedded Figures

Learning Objectives : In this chapter, students will learn about:
- ✓ Identification of a small hidden part
- ✓ Identification of the main figure

CHAPTER SUMMARY

When a figure is embossed on another figure, it is said to be an embedded figure. Embedded figures can be divided into two parts.

1. Identification of a small hidden part in the given figure.
2. Identification of the main figure in which the given part is hidden.

Example 1: Which of the following part is embedded in the given figure?

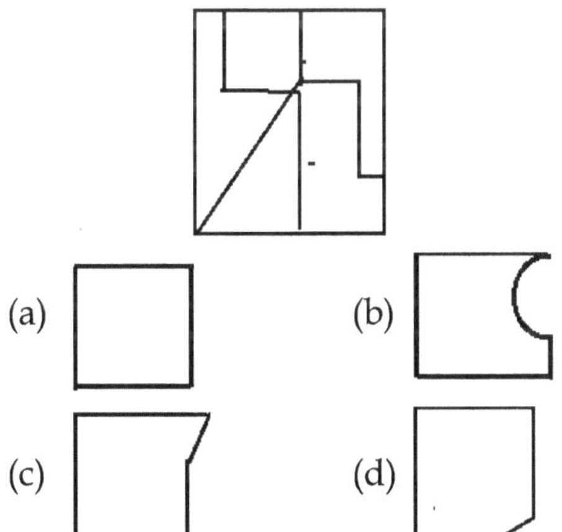

(a)   (b)

(c)   (d)

Sol. (d)

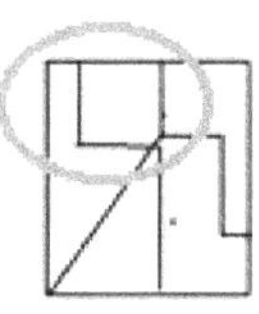

Example 2: In which of the following figures, is the given shape embedded?

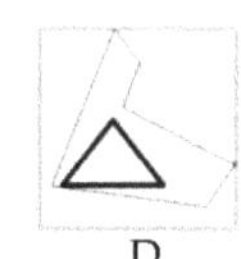

A   B   C   D

Sol. (d)

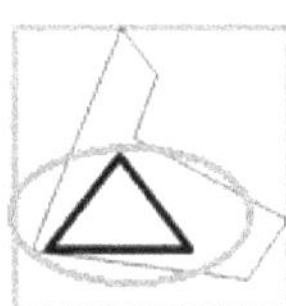

Directions (1–4): Which of the following figures is hidden or embedded in the given figure?

1.

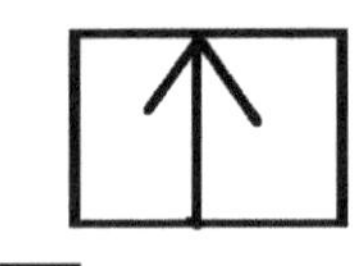

(a)  (b) 

(c) 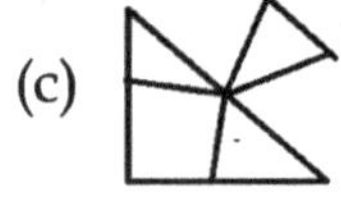 (d) 

2.

(a)  (b) 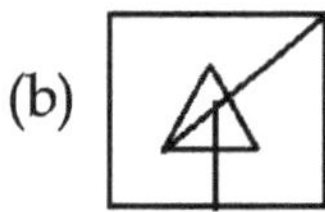

(c)  (d) 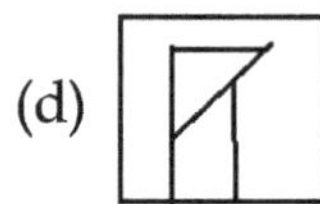

3.

(a) 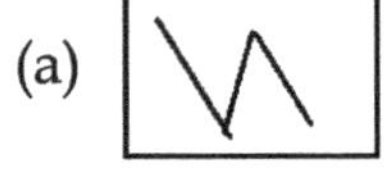 (b) 

(c)  (d) 

4.

(a)  (b) 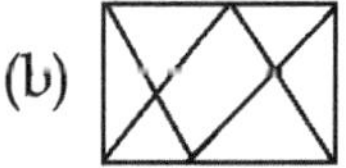

(c)  (d) 

5. Find the figure which is not hidden in the given figure.

(a) 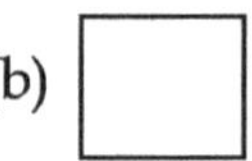 (b) 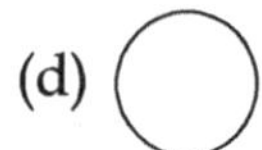

(c)   (d)

6.

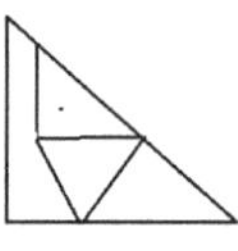

(a) 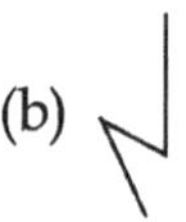 (b)

(c)   (d) 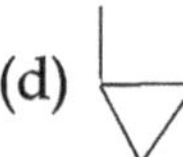

Directions (7–10): In which of the following figures, is the given shape (X) embedded as its part?

7.

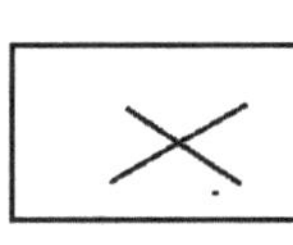 Shape X

(a) 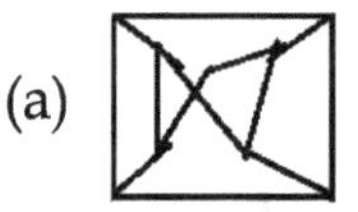 (b)

(c)   (d) 

8.

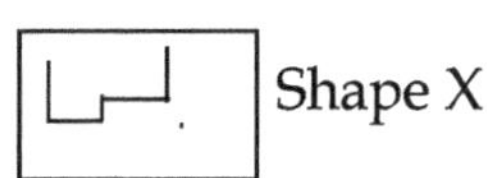 Shape X

(a)   (b) 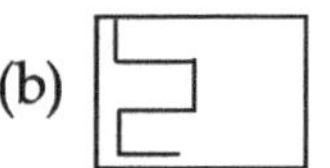

(c)   (d) 

9. 
Shape X

(a)    (b) 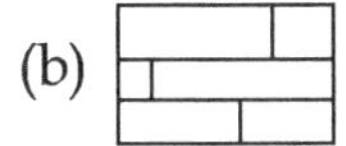

(c) 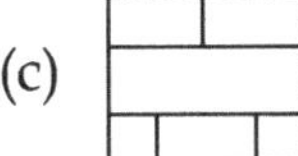   (d) 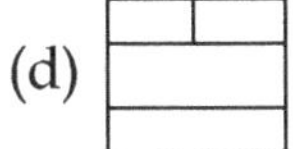

10.  Shape X

(a)    (b) 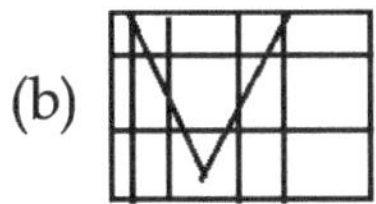

(c)    (d) 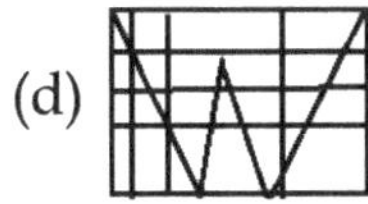

11. Which of the following part is embedded in the given figure?

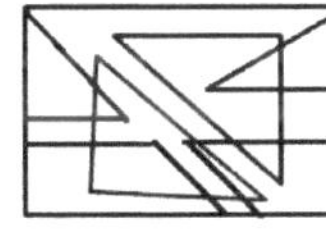

(a) 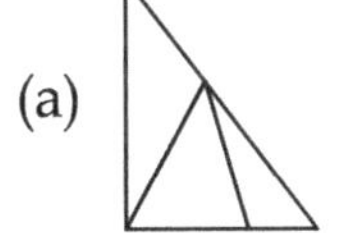   (b) 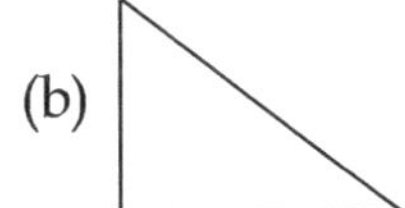

(c) 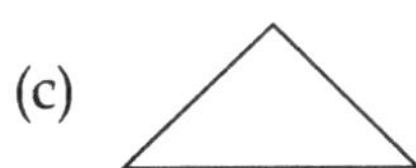   (d) 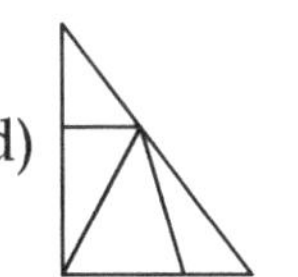

12. Which of the following part is embedded in the given figure?

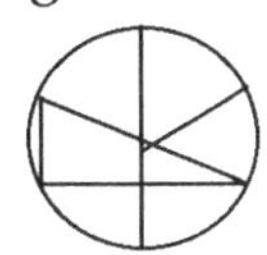

(a)    (b) 

(c)    (d) 

13. In which of the following figures, is the given shape (X) embedded as its part?

(a) 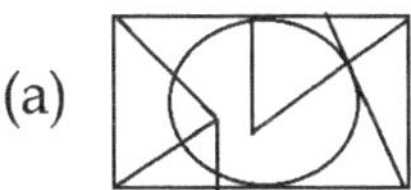   (b) 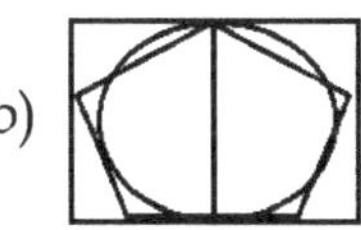

(c) 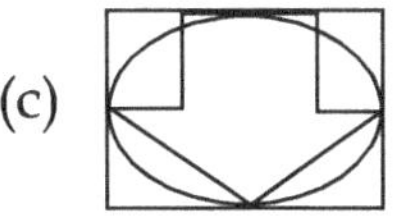   (d) 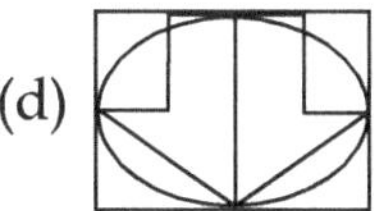

14. In which of the following figures, is the given shape (X) embedded as its part?

(a) 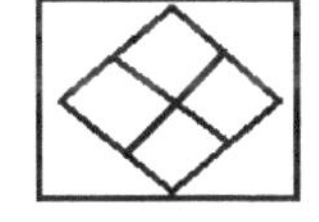   (b) 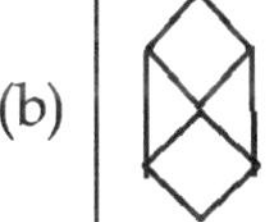

(c) 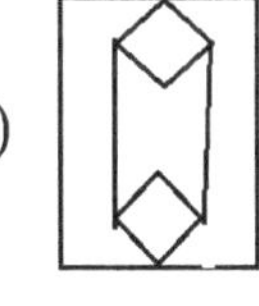   (d) 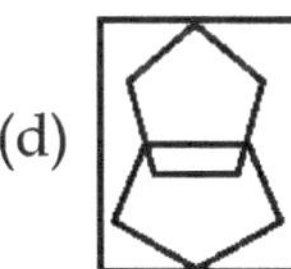

15. In which of the following figures, is the given shape (X) embedded as its part?

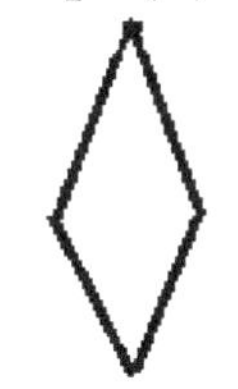 Shape X

(a) 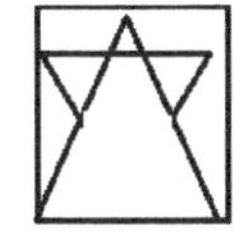   (b) 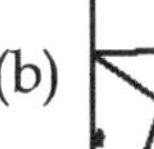

(c)    (d) 

16. Which of the following parts is embedded in the given figure?

(a) 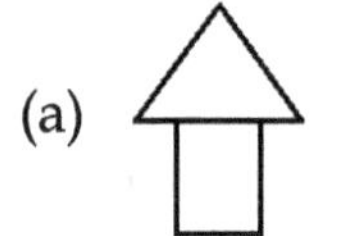   (b) 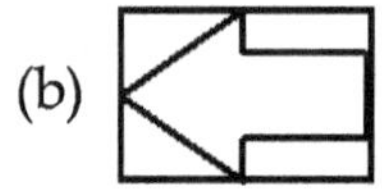

(c)    (d) 

17. In which of the following figures, is the given shape (X) embedded as its part?

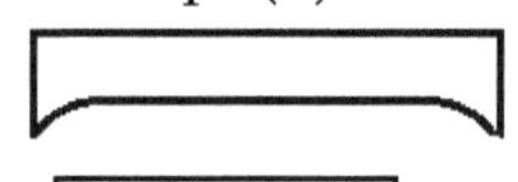 Shape X

(a) 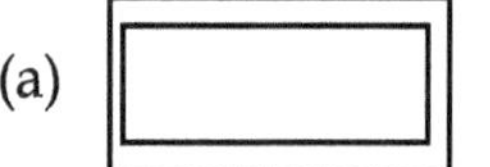   (b) 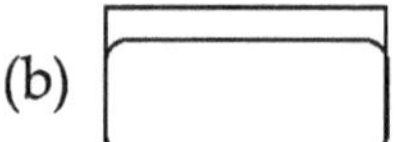

(c)    (d) 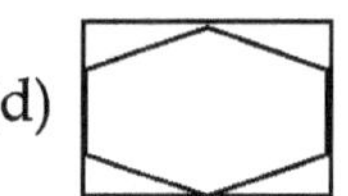

18. In which of the following figures, is the given shape (X) embedded as its part?

(a) 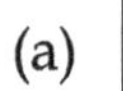   (b) 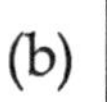

(c) 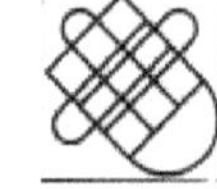   (d)

19. Find the alphabet which is not hidden in the given figure.

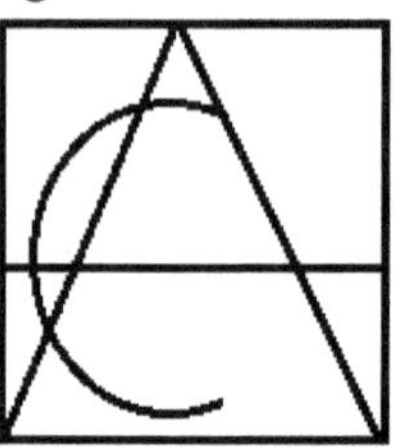

(a) C   (b) A
(c) N   (d) W

20. Look at the following figure carefully.

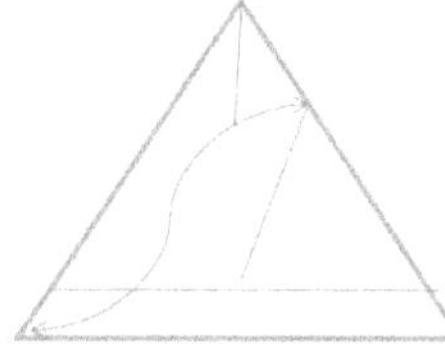

Which of the following figures is hidden or embedded in the given figure?

(a)    (b) 

(c)    (d) 

Grouping of Figures 8

Learning Objectives : In this chapter, students will learn about:
- ✓ Grouping of Figures

CHAPTER SUMMARY

In grouping of figures, a set of figures or numbers are grouped on the basis of certain properties or parameters. The basic fundamentals of fractioning, division and multiplication are applied while grouping of figures.

Example 1: Identify the number of groups of 2 from the following pictures.

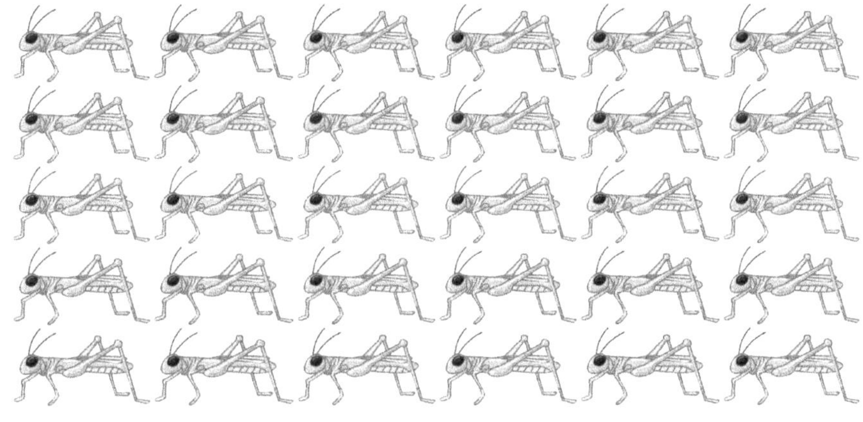

  (a) 10   (b) 15
  (c) 20   (d) 30

Sol. (b)

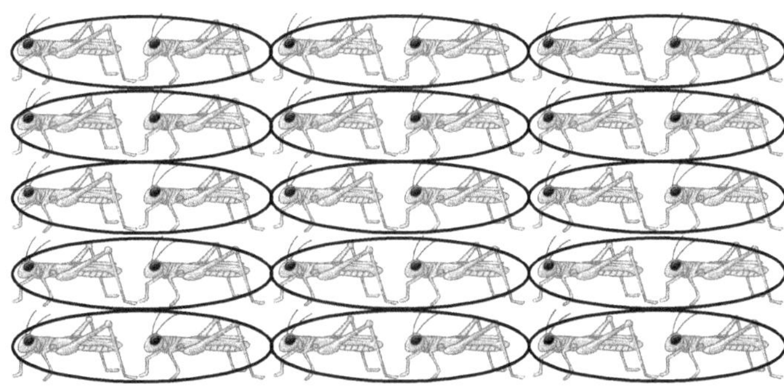

Total 15 groups can be formed.

Example 2: Number 5 belongs to group _______.

<table>
<tr><td>

5, 15, 30, 100, 21

33, 10, 13 19, 28

20, 24, 18, 68, 32

</td><td>

4, 7, 12, 18, 24

28, 7, 9, 38, 42

9, 36, 64, 63, 59

</td><td>

17, 52, 54, 8, 7

51, 41, 31, 21, 11

101, 116, 109, 89, 72

</td></tr>
<tr><td align="center">P Group</td><td align="center">Q Group</td><td align="center">R Group</td></tr>
</table>

   (a) R group   (b) P and Q group

   (c) P group   (d) P, Q and R groups

Sol. (c)

1. How many groups of 3-stars are there?

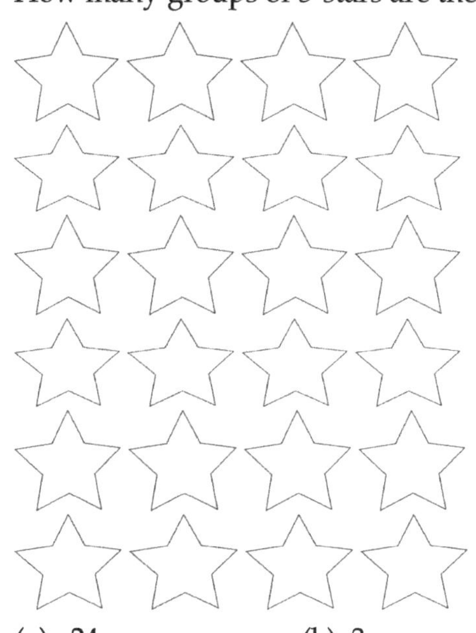

   (a) 24 (b) 3
   (c) 8   (d) 10

2. How many groups of 2 rectangles can be formed from the group of assorted shapes given in the box?

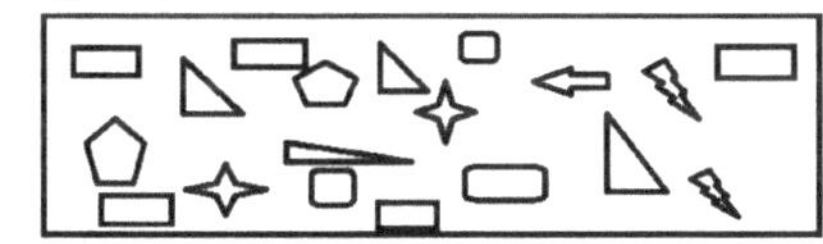

   (a) 1   (b) 2
   (c) 4   (d) 3

3. Identify the group in which components can be divided into groups of four equally and completely.

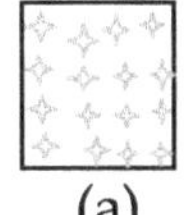 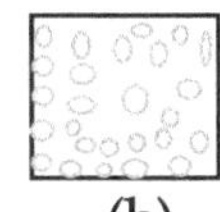  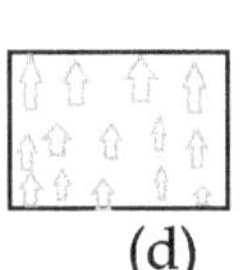

   (a)   (b)   (c)   (d)

4. How many groups of 2 giraffes are there?

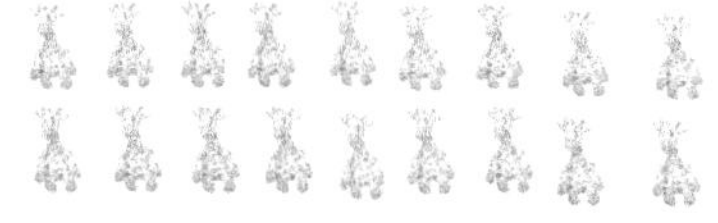

   (a) 10 (b) 9
   (c) 18 (d) 20

5. How many groups of 4 bottles are there?

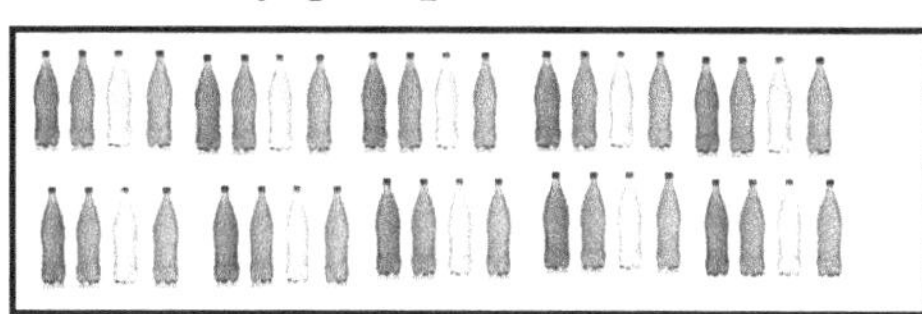

   (a) 10 (b) 5
   (c) 20 (c) 40

6. How many groups of 3 dark bottles can be formed from given group of bottles?

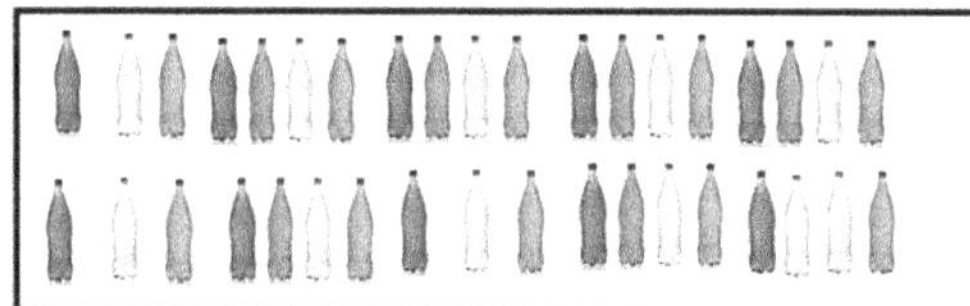

   (a) 5   (b) 10
   (c) 6   (d) 3

7. Shape (A) belongs to group _______.

   Shape A

   Group W   Group X   Group Y   Group Z

 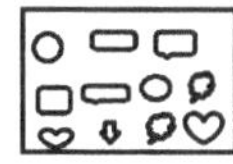 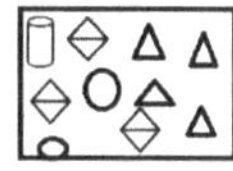 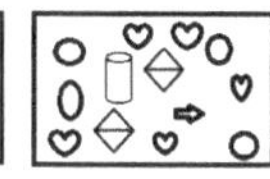

   (a) Only W
   (b) Only Z
   (c) Both W and X
   (d) Both W and Y

Direction (8–11): Observe and study the given figures and choose the correct answer which relates to the given figures.

8. 

   (a) 5 groups of 2 fish
   (b) 2 groups of 5 fish
   (c) 3 groups of 5 fish
   (d) 2 groups of 6 fish

9. 

(a) 4 groups of dark and 4 groups of light fish

(b) 3 groups of dark and 4 groups of light fish

(c) 5 groups of dark and 4 groups of light fish

(d) None of these

10.

(a) 3 groups of 3 apples and 2 groups of 3 pears

(b) 2 groups of 3 apples, 2 groups of 3 pineapples, and 2 groups of 3 pears

(c) 2 groups of 3 apples, 2 groups of 3 pineapples, 1 group of 3 bananas, and 2 groups of 3 pears

(d) 3 groups of 3 apples, 3 groups of 3 pineapples, 1 group of 3 bananas, and 2 groups of 3 pears

11.

(a) 5 groups of 5 tigers
(b) 5 groups of 2 tigers
(c) 10 groups of 2 tigers
(d) 12 groups of 5 tigers

12. How many groups of 3 carrots can be formed from given group of carrots?

(a) 3   (b) 5
(c) 6   (d) 4

13. The numbers related to 3 belong to which group?

Group X	Group Y	Group Z
4, 6, 8, 10, 12 20, 21, 23, 25 27, 30, 28, 32	3, 9, 21, 12, 28 15, 18, 17, 16 27, 30, 24, 36	12, 11, 10, 9, 7 99, 23, 22, 26, 25 100, 101, 201 301, 1

(a) Only X
(b) Both X and Y
(c) Only Z
(d) All three, X, Y and Z

14. How many bunches of 4 grapes each can be formed from the given bunches of grapes? [Each given bunch has 8 grapes in it, at present.]

(a) 12   (b) 6
(c) 8   (d) 20

15. How many groups of 4 cockroaches can be formed from the given group of cockroaches?

(a) 3   (b) 5
(c) 4   (d) 6

16. How many more eggs are required if we want to form 3 groups of 6 eggs?

(a) 4
(b) 7
(c) 8
(d) 10

Direction (17–18): Look at the figure given below and answer the following questions.

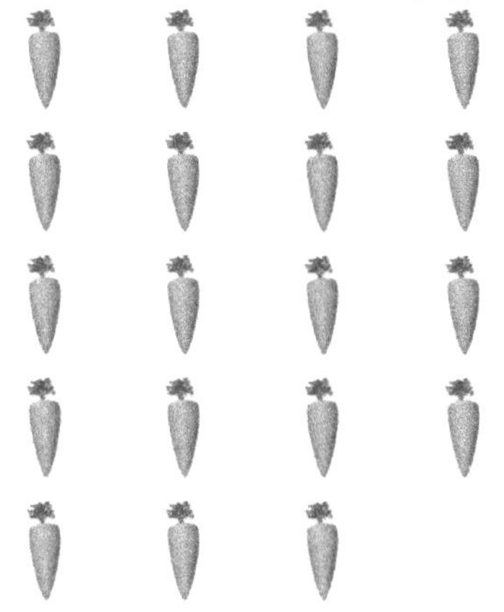

17. How many groups of 4 butterflies can be formed?

(a) 4
(b) 5
(c) 8
(d) 6

18. How many groups of 8 butterflies can be formed?

(a) 4
(b) 2
(c) 5
(d) 7

19. How many more triangles are required if we want to make 4 groups of 3 triangles?

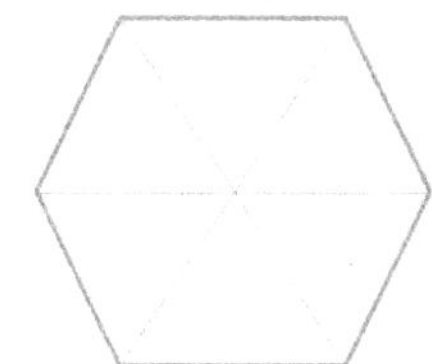

(a) 4
(b) 6
(c) 8
(d) 3

20. How many more triangles are required to complete 6 groups of 2 triangles?

(a) 4
(b) 3
(c) 5
(d) 6

Measuring Units 9

Learning Objectives : In this chapter, students will learn about:
- ✓ Length
- ✓ Mass
- ✓ Volume
- ✓ Money

CHAPTER SUMMARY

Measurement is related to counting or measuring an object. The parameters of measurement are: length, weight, volume, time and money.

For example,

1. Length of an object is measured in meter (m) or centimeter (cm).

   1 meter = 100 cm

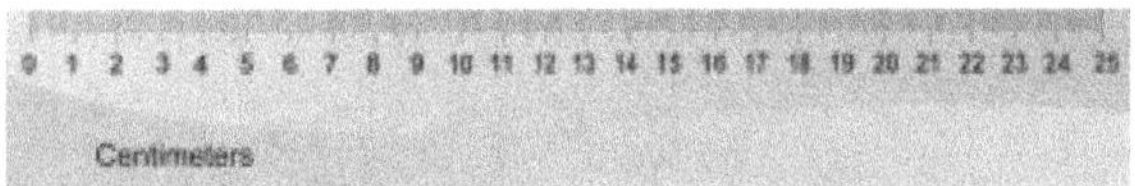

2. Mass of an object is measured in kilogram (kg) or gram (gm).

   1 kg = 1000 g.

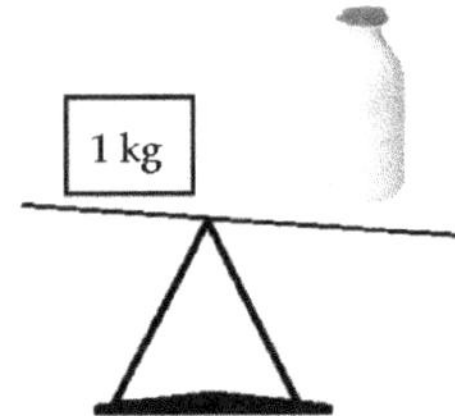

3. Volume is the amount of liquid, for example, water, juice, milk, in a container. Volume is measured in litre (l) or millilitre (ml).

4. We use a clock or a watch to check the time. Time is measured in hours, minutes and second.

   There are 60 minutes (min) in 1 hour (h).

   1 hour = 60 minutes

   1 minute = 60 seconds (sec)

   1 day = 24 hours (h)

   1 week = 7 days

   1 month = 4 weeks

   1 year = 12 months (365 days)

5. Money is measured in Rupee in India.

   1 Rupee = 100 Paise

   Symbol of Rupee = ₹

Example 1: How many Paise are there in 5 Rupees?

Sol. 1 Rupee = 100 Paise

   100 * 5 = 500

   So, there are 500 Paise in 5 Rupees.

Example 2: Look at the figure carefully and answer the following question.

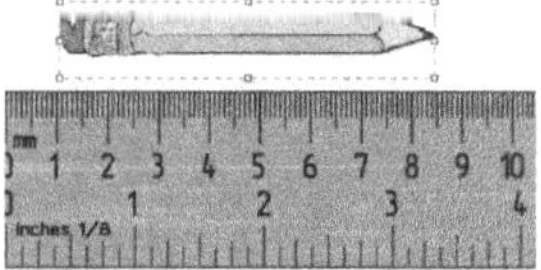

The pencil is _______ cm long.

(a) 8   (b) 8.5

(c) 7.5   (d) 7

Sol. (c)

Example 3: Look at the figure carefully and answer the following question.

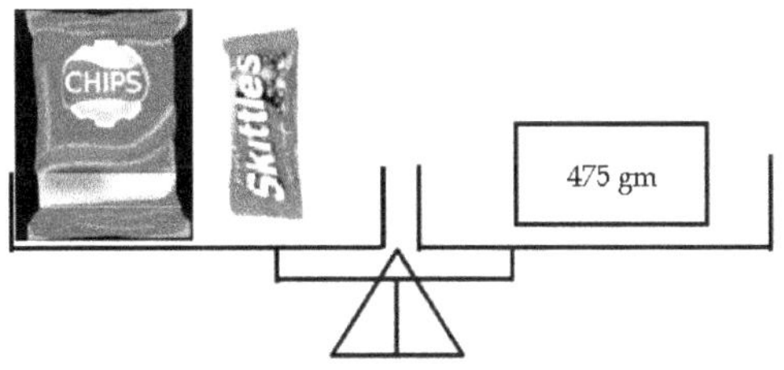

The total mass (weight) of a packet of chips and packet of sweets is 475 gm. The mass of the sweet packet is 250 gm. What is the weight of the chips packet?

(a) 200 gm   (B 225 gm

(c) 250 gm   (d) 325 gm

Sol. (b)

Total weight = 475 gm, weight of the packet of sweets = 250 gm, so weight of the chips packet = 475 − 250 = 225 gm.

Example 4: Look at the figure carefully and answer the following question.

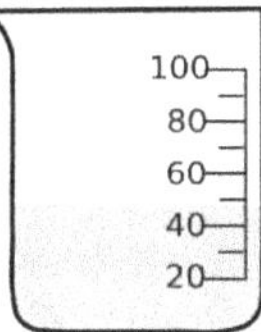

The beaker contains _____ ml of water.

(a) 100   (b) 40

(c) 45   (d) 50

Sol. (d)

Example 5: How many days are there in 5 weeks?

(a) 35   (b) 36

(c) 25   (d) 37

Sol. (a)

1 week = 7 days, so 5 weeks = 5 * 7 = 35 days.

Example 6: Sumit earns ₹500 per day, so how many rupees will he earn in 30 days?

(a) ₹1500   (b) ₹15000

(c) ₹10000   (d) ₹20000

Sol. (b)

One day = ₹500, so in 30 days = 30 * 500 = ₹15000.

Directions (1-4): Study the picture and answer the following questions.

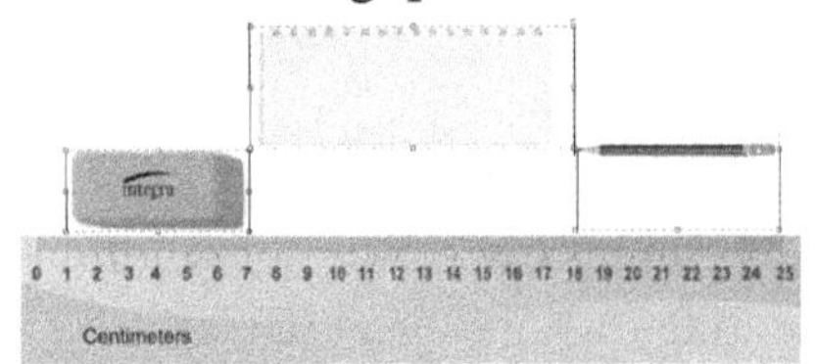

1. The length of the eraser is _______ cm.
   (a) 7   (b) 6
   (c) 6.5   (d) 9
2. The length of the pencil is _______ cm.
   (a) 6   (b) 8
   (c) 7   (d) 7.5
3. Eraser is _____ cm shorter than the pencil.
   (a) 1 cm   (b) 3 cm
   (c) 2 cm   (d) 0.5 cm
4. The length of the notebook is _______ cm.
   (a) 18   (b) 11
   (c) 12   (d) 13
5. Look at the figure carefully and answer the following question.

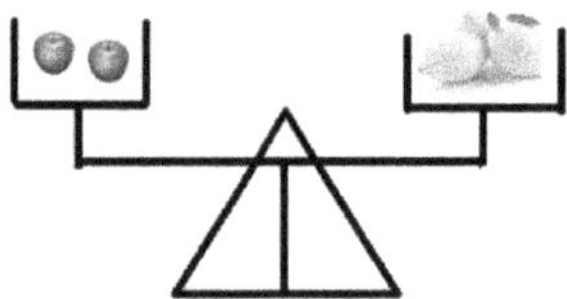

   If the weight of two apples is 250 grams, and all the three lemons are of same weight, then what is the weight of one lemon?
   (a) 75.55   (b) 73.33
   (c) 83.33   (d) 85.33
6. Look at the figure carefully and answer the following question.

   Which is the heaviest?
   (a) Grapes   (b) Pineapple
   (c) Apple   (d) Banana

Directions (7–8): Look at pictures carefully and answer the following questions.

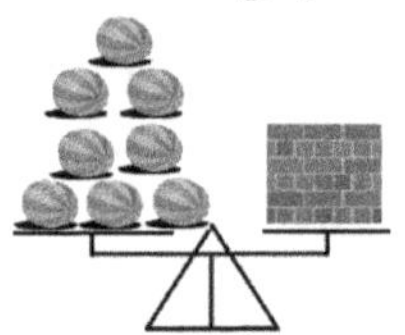

7. If one is equal to 1000 grams, what would be the weight of bricks?
   (a) 2000 gm   (b) 10000 gm
   (c) 8000 gm   (d) 25000 gm
8. If one is equal to 1000 grams, what would be the total weight of water melon and bricks?
   (a) 4000 gm   (b) 2000 gm
   (c) 8000 gm   (d) 16000 gms

Directions (9–10): Look at the pictures carefully and answer the following questions.

9. The tree is _______ m tall.
   (a) 25   (b) 50
   (c) 55   (d) 23.6
10. The boy is ______ m tall.
   (a) 23.6   (b) 55 m
   (c) 1.4 m   (d) 1.5 m

Direction (11–13): Look at the pictures carefully and answer the following questions.

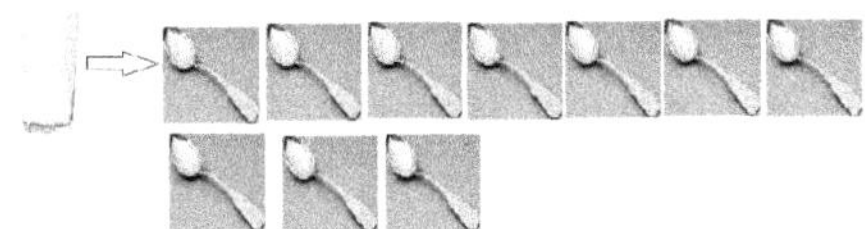

11. If three glasses is equal to 500 ml, then the jug can hold _______ ml of water.
    (a) 950 (b) 850
    (c) 750 (d) 1000

12. If one table spoon is equal to 15 ml, then 1 glass is equal to _______.
    (a) 250 (b) 150
    (c) 100 (d) 125

13. A jug is filled with eight glasses and one glass is filled with 10 table spoons, then how many spoons can fill a jug?
    (a) 80 (b) 70
    (c) 100 (d) 180

14. If 750 ml of milk is required to prepare 500 gm of curd, then how much milk is required to prepare 2000 gm of curd?
    (a) 3500 (b) 2000
    (c) 2500 (d) 3000

Direction: A vase of water can fill up 6 cups. A bucket of water can fill up 12 cups. A tub of water can fill 24 cups.

Based on the above information, answer the following questions.

15. Somya needs _______ vases to fill up two buckets.
    (a) 2 (b) 3
    (c) 5 (d) 4

16. Somya needs _______ vase(s) and _______ buckets(s) to fill up a tub of water.
    (a) 2, 4 (b) 3, 4
    (c) 4, 2 (d) 4, 1

17. Somya goes for music classes at 3.30 pm every day. The time being shown by the wall clock now is

How much time is left for her class now?
    (a) 60 minutes (b) 90 minutes
    (c) 100 minutes (d) 110 minutes

18. Which clock shows half past 10?
    (a) 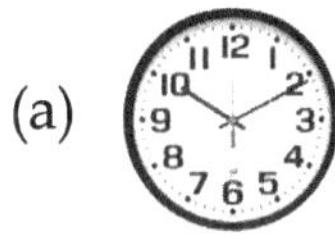 (b) 
    (c)  (d) 

19. How much time does the hour hand of a clock take to complete three rounds?
    (a) 60 minutes (b) 1 hour
    (c) 180 minutes (d) 2 hours

20. How many minutes are there in one day?
    (a) 1440 (b) 550
    (c) 1660 (d) 1760

21. Sanjay takes 10 minutes to complete writing one page. How much minutes does he take to complete writing 6 pages?
    (a) 600 (b) 60
    (c) 65 (d) 76

Direction (22–24): Study the given table below carefully and answer the following questions.

Item	Price
	₹75
	₹175
	₹100
	₹100
	₹45

22. Shruti wants to buy 1 notebook, 2 geometry boxes and 2 sets of colour pencils. She needs _______ altogether.

(a) ₹450   (b) ₹390

(c) ₹515   (d) ₹445

23. Anaya wants to buy 1 water bottle, 1 lunch box and 1 notebook. She has ₹200. How much more money she needs to buy all these items?

(a) ₹100   (b) ₹175

(c) ₹75   (d) ₹200

24. Vinay bought a textbook and he gave the cashier ₹100. He receives ₹_____ change.

(a) ₹20   (b) ₹25

(c) ₹50   (d) ₹55

25. Look at the given fruit box. It has 16 fruits. Each fruit cost ₹3. How much does 5 fruit boxes cost?

(a) ₹240   (b) ₹440

(c) ₹550   (d) ₹300

Geometrical Shapes 10

Learning Objectives : In this chapter, students will learn about:
- ✓ Geometrical Lines
- ✓ Plane Geometrical Shapes
- ✓ Solid Geometrical Shapes

CHAPTER SUMMARY

Shape is defined as an external boundary or an outline of an object. An outline that provides the geometric information is called the geometric shape of an object.

There are several kinds of shapes around us. We can observe them in our daily life also. Some of them are described below.

Geometrical Lines

Vertical Line
A line that moves from up to down, on a page is called the vertical line.

Horizontal Line
A line that moves from left to right across the page is called a horizontal line.

Slanting Line
A line that is straight but leans (/) towards another direction is known as a slanting line.

Curved Line
A line which is not straight and has no sharp edges is called a curve line or a curve.

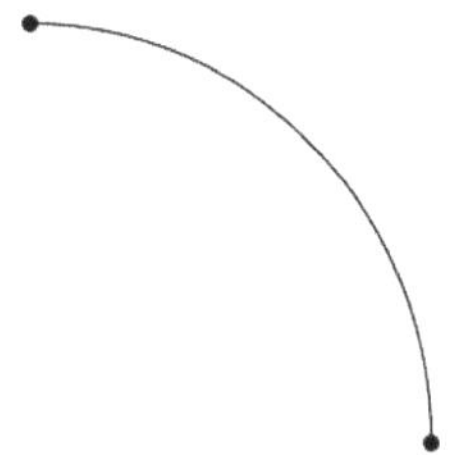

Example 1: Which two types of geometrical lines form the figure shown below?

(a) Four vertical lines
(b) Two vertical and two horizontal lines
(c) One vertical and one slanting line
(d) Four slanting lines

Sol. (b)
There are two vertical and two horizontal lines in the given figure.

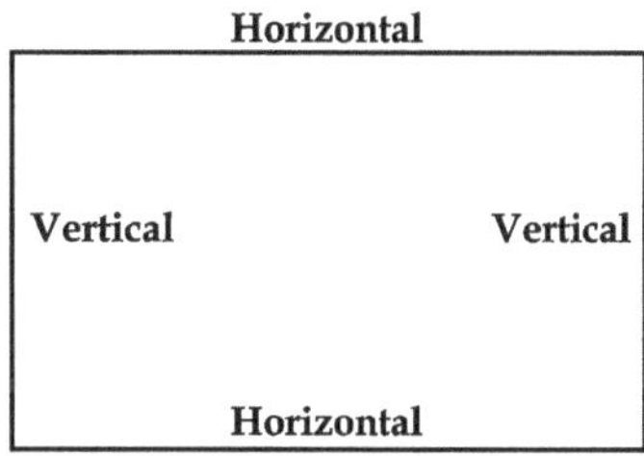

Example 2: Count the curved lines in the given figure.

(a) Six (b) Two
(c) Five (d) Four

Sol. (c)
There are five curved lines in the given figure.

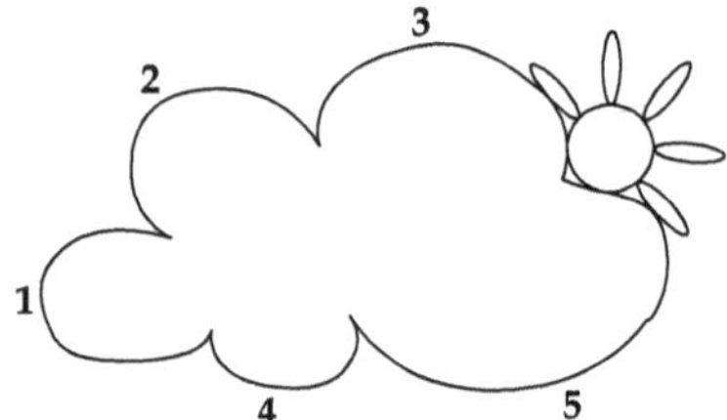

Plane Geometrical Shapes

Triangle
Triangle is a shape, which has three sides or edges. Triangles may vary according to the sizes of the sides, for example: A triangle with three equal sides, a triangle with unequal sides.

Square
A shape that has four equally-sized sides is called a square. It looks like a box.

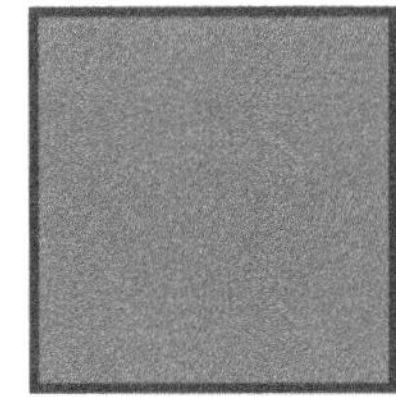

Rectangle
Rectangle also looks like a box. It has four sides, with two sets of equal sides, which are opposite to each other.

Circle
It is a round figure with no corners.

Solid Geometrical Shapes

Cone
A cone has two faces, one is curved and another is plane. It has one corner. Shape of a cone is similar to the triangle but it has a circle as a base.

Cylinder
A cylinder has three faces, one curved surface along with two plane surfaces. It has no corners.

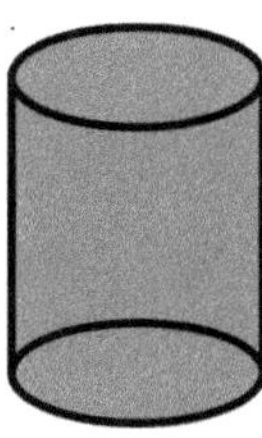

Cube
A shape with six square faces, 12 edges and 8 corners is called a cube. It resembles a carton.

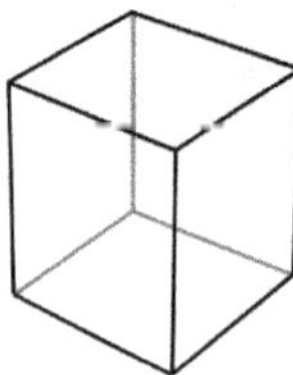

Cuboid

Cuboid is a shape with six-plane-rectangle faces and eight corners. It has 12 edges.

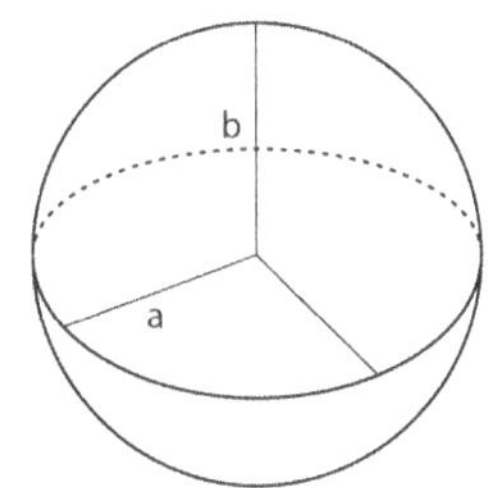

Sphere

Sphere has only one face with no edges or corners.

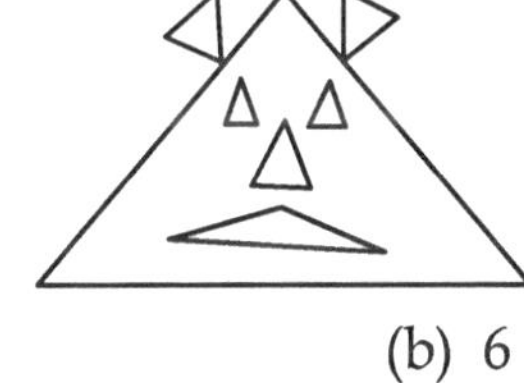

Example 1: Count the number of triangles in the given figure.

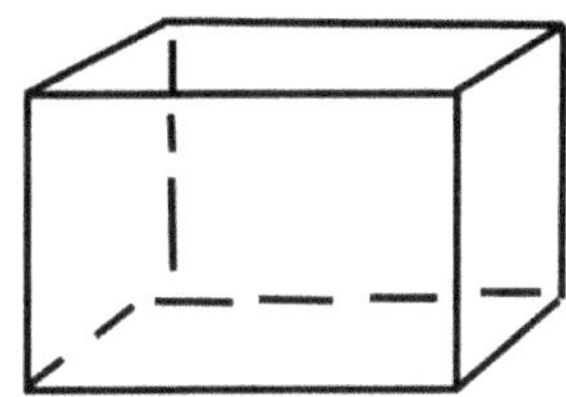

   (a) 7   (b) 6

   (c) 8   (d) 5

Sol. (a)

There are seven triangles in the given figure.

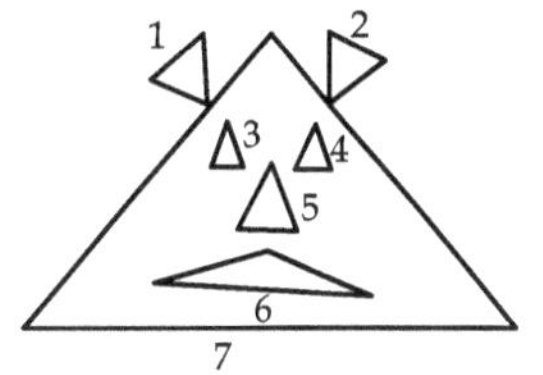

Example 2: The following figure is made up of _______ number of squares and _______ number of rectangles.

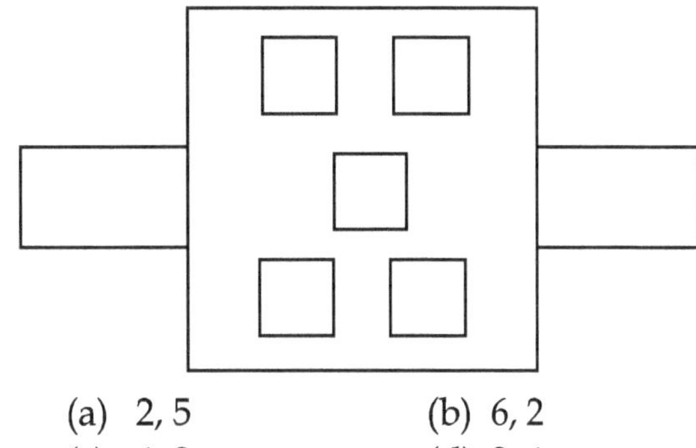

   (a) 2, 5   (b) 6, 2

   (c) 4, 2   (d) 2, 4

Sol. (b)

The figure is made up of six squares and two rectangles.

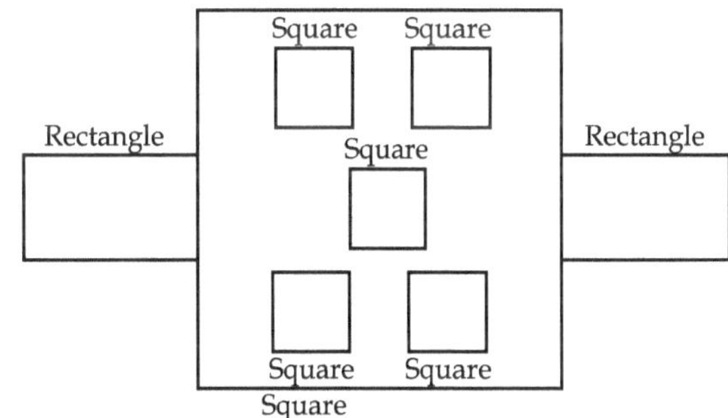

1. The figure given below is made up of ______ triangles.

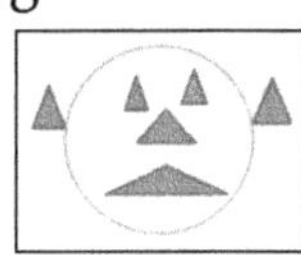

   (a) 5   (b) 6
   (c) 7   (d) 8

2. Which two shapes form the given figure?

   (a) Rhombus and square
   (b) Triangle and square
   (c) Kite and rhombus
   (d) Rectangle and triangle

3. Which two types of geometrical shapes are hidden in the given picture?

   (a) Square and cylinder
   (b) Rectangle and cylinder
   (c) Cubes and cylinder
   (d) Rectangle and cubes

4. How many lines are not straight lines in the given figure?

   (a) 11   (b) 10
   (c) 9   (d) 3

5. How many circles are there in the given face?

   (a) 1   (b) 2
   (c) 3   (d) 4

6. How many triangles are there in the given figure?

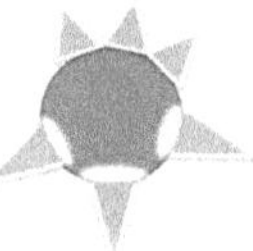

   (a) 6   (b) 3
   (c) 2   (d) 5

7. There are ______ number of ______ in the given figure.

   (a) 6, squares   (b) 6, rectangles
   (c) 4, squares   (d) 4, rectangles

8. Which of the following shape(s) cannot be found in the given figure?

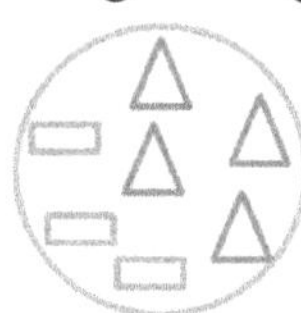

   (a) Circle   (b) Triangle
   (c) Square   (d) Rectangle

9. How many standing lines are there in the given figure?

   (a) 4   (b) 3
   (c) 6   (d) 5

10. Which two shapes do not meet?

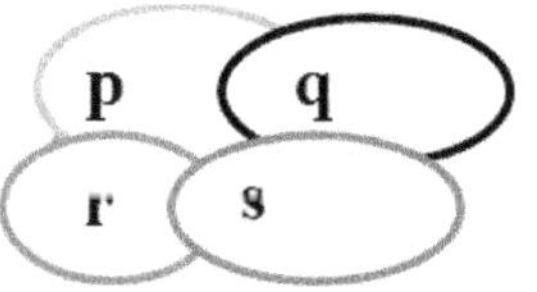

   (a) p and q   (b) q and r
   (c) p and s   (d) p and r

11. How many circles are there in the given figure?

(a) 10   (b) 21
(c) 22   (d) 19

12. Which of the following shapes has the largest number of sides?

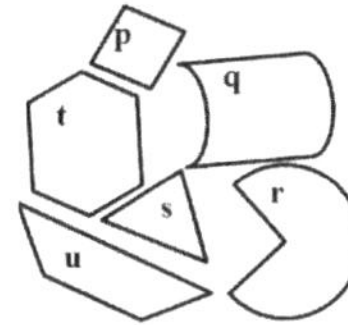

(a) p   (b) q
(c) t   (d) s

13. There are _______ more squares than the triangles in the given figure.

(a) 4   (b) 6
(c) 5   (d) 2

14. How many slanting lines are there in the given figure?

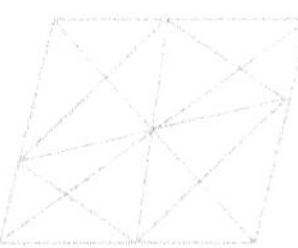

(a) 10   (b) 9
(c) 8   (d) 12

15. The following figure is made up of _______ number of circles.

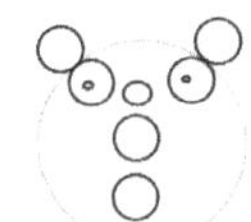

(a) 15   (b) 8
(c) 10   (d) 9

16. Count the number of straight lines, curved lines and circles.

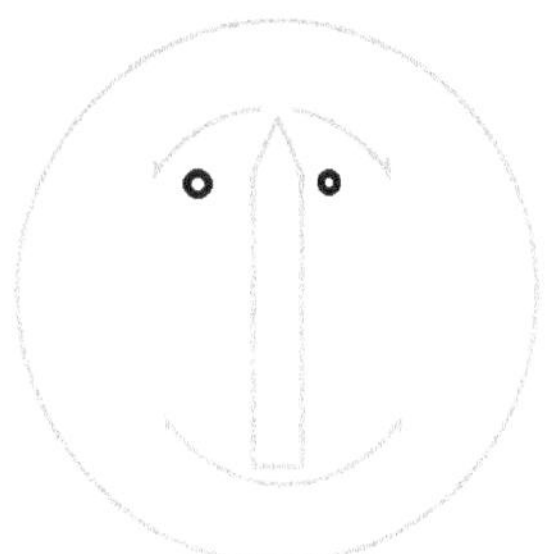

	Straight line	Curved Line	Circle
(a)	2	3	3
(b)	3	3	3
(c)	3	3	1
(d)	3	3	2

17. The given figure is made up of _______ number of curved lines.

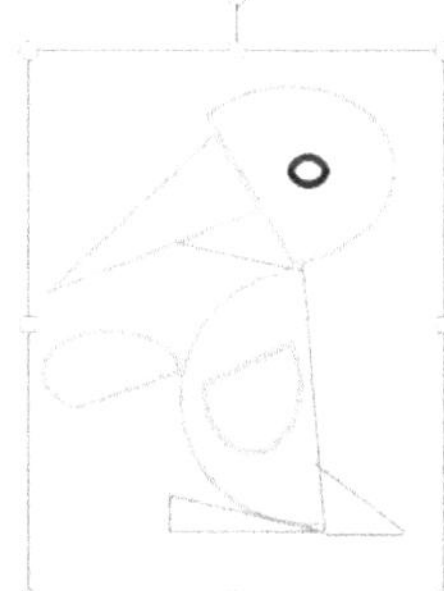

(a) 4   (b) 3
(c) 2   (d) 1

18. How many squares are there in the given figure?

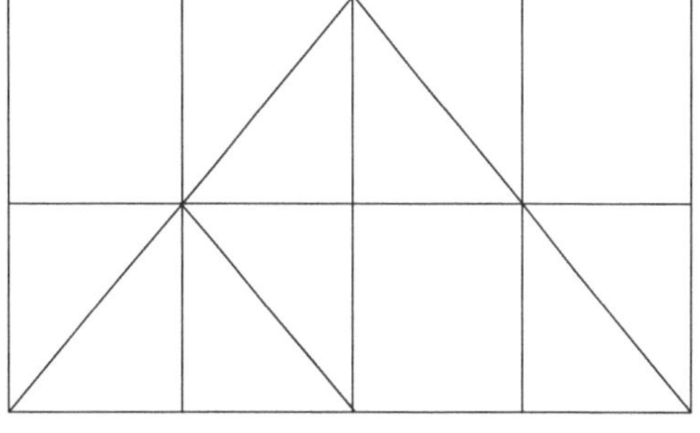

(a) 4   (b) 11
(c) 8   (d) 6

19. Identify the shapes in the figure given below.

(a) Circle, rectangle, triangle, square and Lines
(b) Circle, triangle, and square
(c) Circle, rectangle, and triangle
(d) Circle and rectangle

20. How many triangles are there in the given figure?

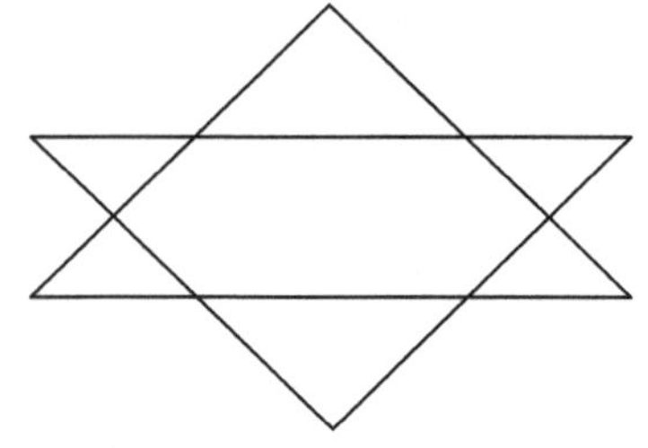

(a) 6   (b) 5
(c) 8   (d) 9

SECTION 3
ACHIEVER'S SECTION

Zip File

A zip file is a way of **grouping**, or **archiving**, multiple files so they act like one file. For example, let's say you want to email a folder of Word documents to someone. You could attach each file individually, but it would take a long time—especially if there are a lot of documents. A better solution would be to put all of the files into a zip file, and then **attach the zip file** to your email.

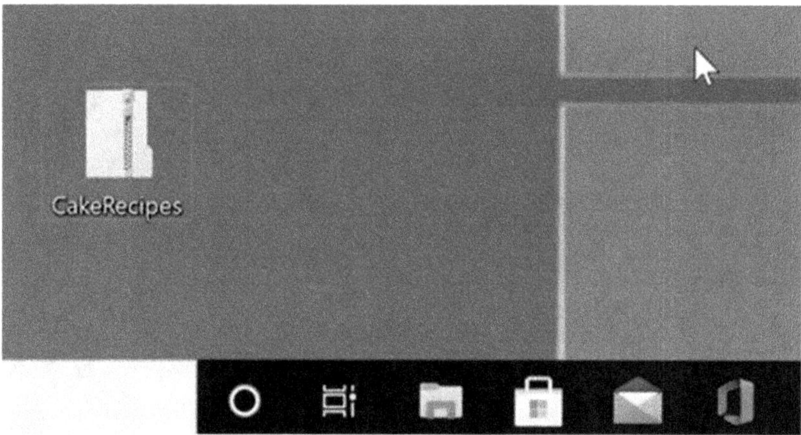

Creating Zip Files

You don't need additional software to create and open zip files. That's because the basic zip file features are built into the operating system.

To create a zip file in Windows:

1. Select the files you want to add to the zip file.

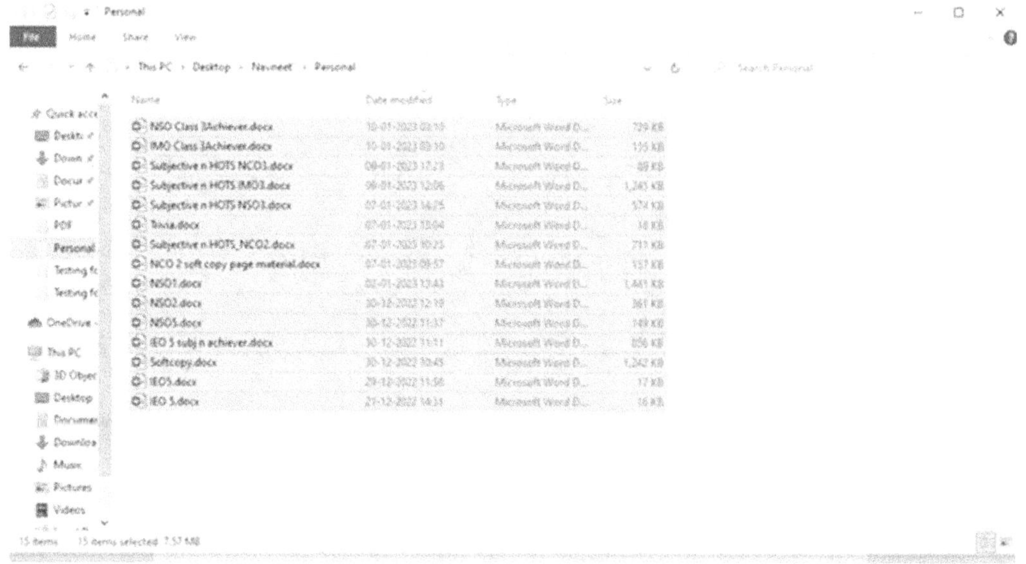

2. Right-click one of the files. A menu will appear.

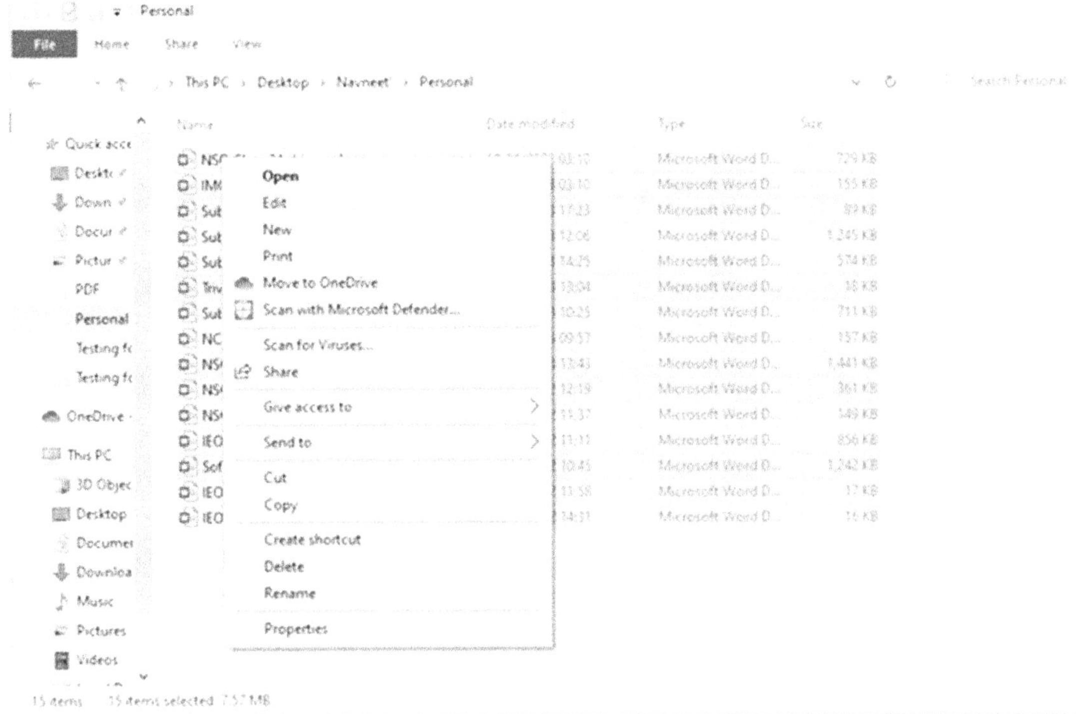

3. In the menu, click Send to and select Compressed (zipped) folder.

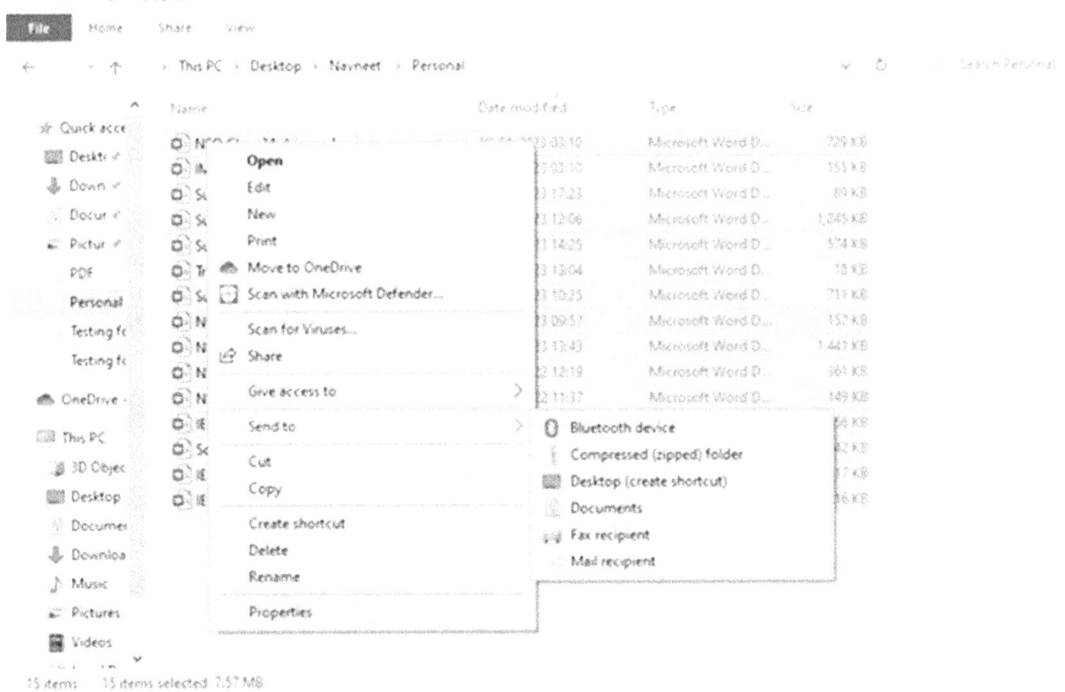

4. A Zip file will appear. If you want, you can type a new name for the zip file.

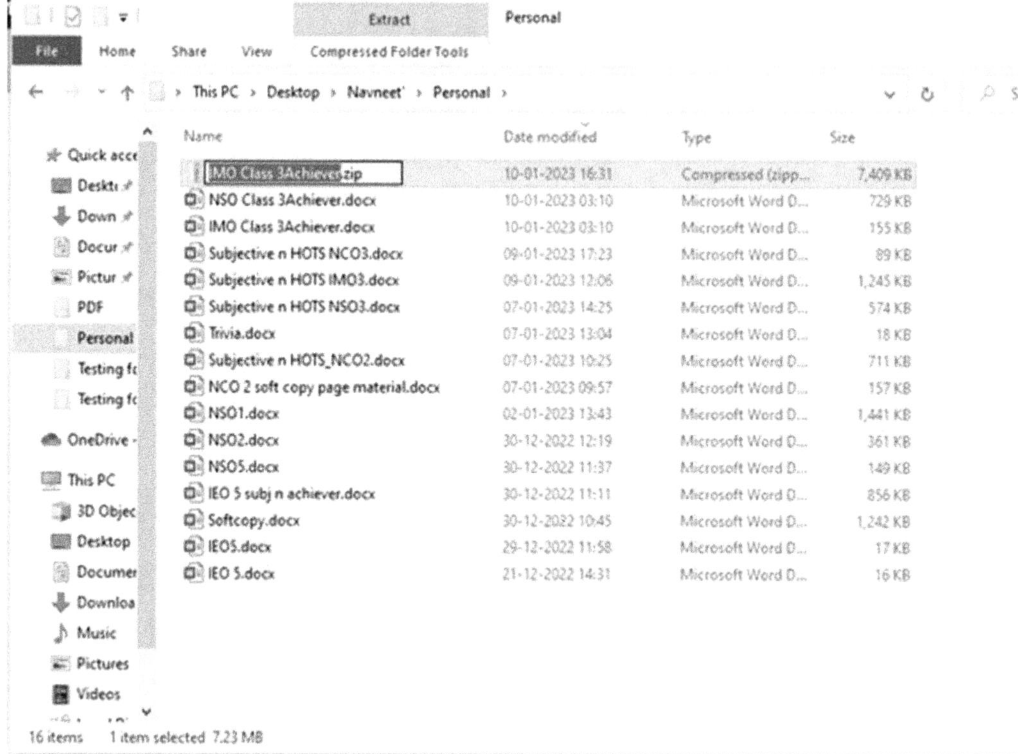

In Windows, once you've created a zip file you can then add more files to it by dragging them onto the zip file's icon.

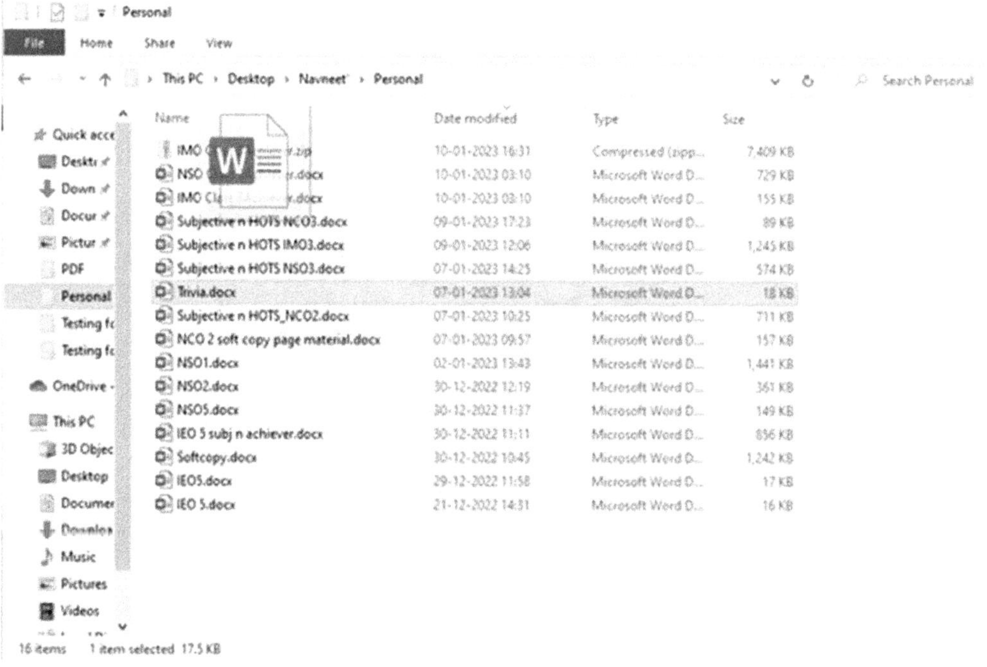

Tips for creating Strong Passwords

A strong password is one that's easy for you to remember but difficult for others to guess. Let's take a look at some of the most important things to consider when creating a password.

- Never use personal information such as your name, birthday, username, or email address. This type of information is often publicly available, which makes it easier for someone to guess your password.
- Use a longer password. Your password should be at least six characters long, although for extra security it should be even longer.
- Don't use the same password for each account. If someone discovers your password for one account, all of your other accounts will be vulnerable.
- Try to include numbers, symbols, and both uppercase and lowercase letters.
- Avoid using words that can be found in the dictionary. For example, swimming1 would be a weak password.
- Random passwords are the strongest. If you're having trouble creating one, you can use a password generator (like http://strongpasswordgenerator.com/) instead.

How to use your smartphone as an alarm clock

For Android devices, the built-in Clock app can schedule one-time alarms and weekly repeating alarms. It's possible to create multiple alarms and turn them on or off individually.

Click the buttons in the interactive below to learn more about the Clock app's features.

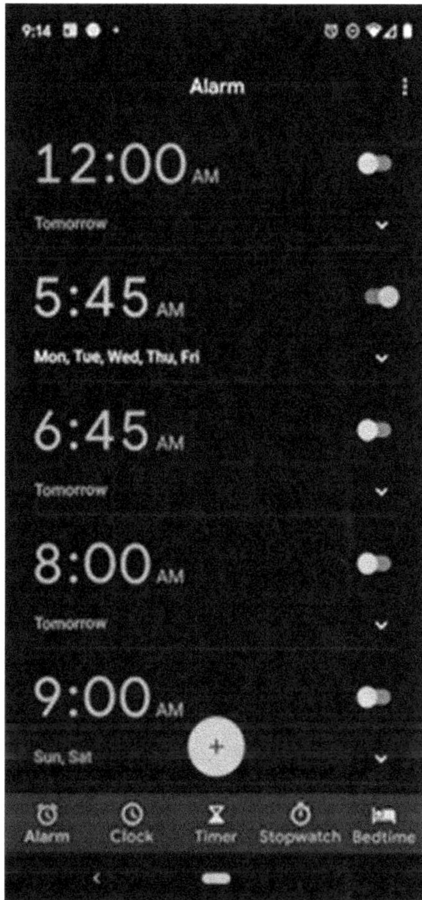

Each alarm can be customized further by changing the alarm sound, labelling the alarm, and setting it to repeat on certain days of the week. Tap the down arrow at the bottom-right of a scheduled alarm to see these additional settings.

Click the buttons in the interactive below to learn more about additional settings for scheduled alarms.

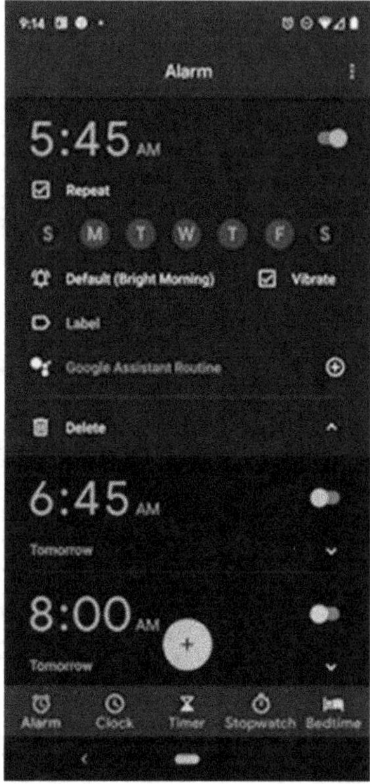

When you create a new alarm or tap an existing alarm to edit it, a screen with a clock face will appear, allowing you to set the time of the alarm.

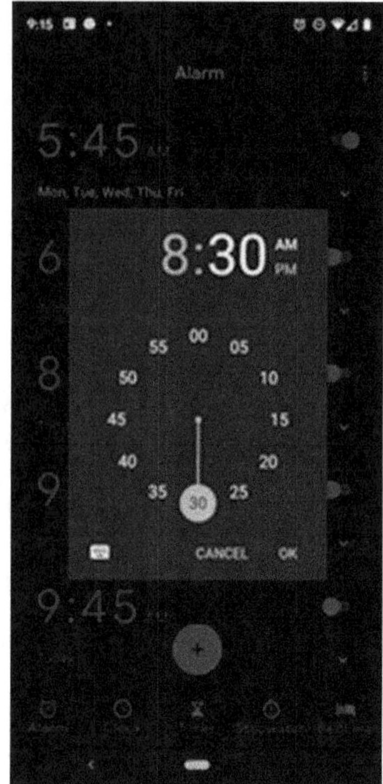

Reasoning

1. What is the missing number?

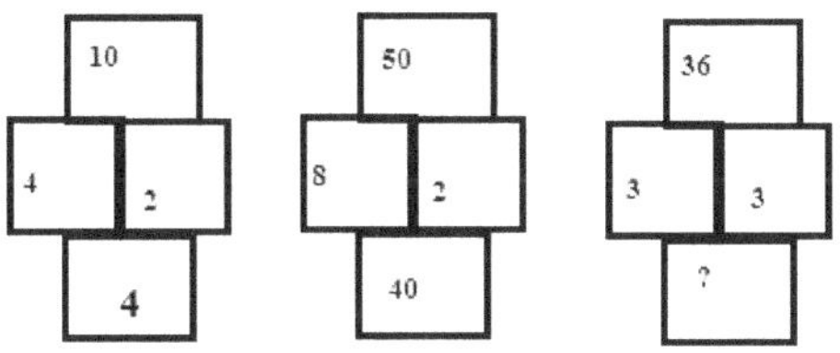

  (a) 32   (b) 42
  (c) 30   (d) 33

2. Find the odd one out.

  (a) ABCE   (b) 

  (c)   (d)

3. How many slanting lines are there in the given figure?

  (a) 14   (b) 20
  (c) 18   (d) 12

4. Match column-I with column-II to get the sum of the numbers as 50.

Column-I	Column-II
(i) 22	(a) 25
(ii) 15	(b) 28
(iii) 25	(c) 35
(iv) 45	(d) 5

  (a) i-b, ii-c, iii-a, iv-d
  (b) i- a, ii-c, iii-b, iv-d
  (c) i-b, ii-d, iii-a, iv-c
  (d) i-c, ii-b, iii-d, iv-a

5. Use the skip-counting method to find the missing numbers.

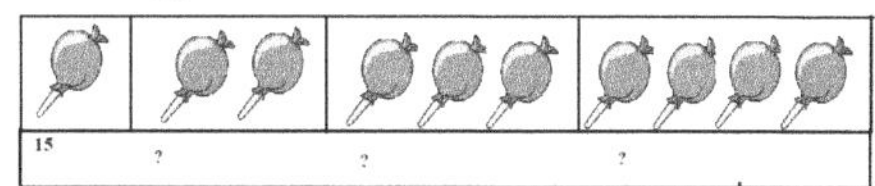

  Value of 1 candy = 15
  (a) 45, 60, 90   (b) 15, 40, 55
  (c) 40, 55, 60   (d) 30, 45, 60

6. Look at the number cloud. The lowest 4 digit number that can be formed without repeating the digits is _______.

  (a) 2015   (b) 1025
  (c) 1250   (d) 2150

7. The given figure is made up of _______ straight lines and _______ curved lines, respectively.

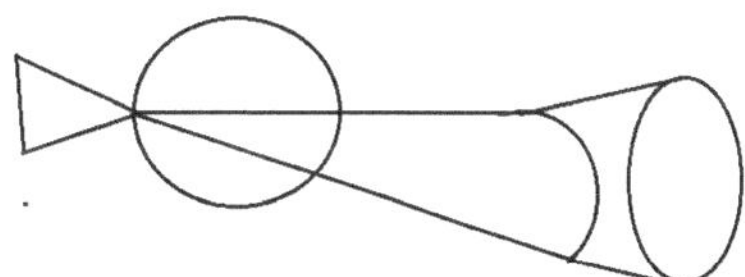

  (a) 7, 6   (b) 6, 7
  (c) 7, 8   (d) 5, 6

8. The given picture shows _______.

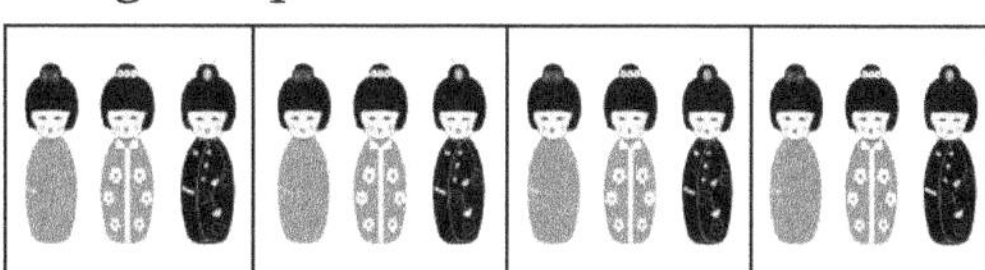

  (a) 3 groups of 3 dolls
  (b) 4 groups of 4 dolls
  (c) 4 groups of 3 dolls
  (d) 3 groups of 4 dolls

9. Rohit and Sonia are going to visit their grandparents in their village and then they will go to a hill station for holidays. They have made (✓) and (✦) marks on the calendar for the days they will spend with their grandparents and in the hill station, respectively.

   How many days will they spend in the hill station (I) and with their grandparents (II), respectively?

June						
Mon	Tue	Wed	Thu	Fri	Sat	Sun
	1	2	3	4	5	6
7	8	9	10	11	12	13
14	15 ✓	16 ✓	17 ✓	18 ✓	19 ✓	20 ✓
21 ✦	22 ✦	23 ✦	24 ✦	25	26	27
28	29	30				

	I	II
(a)	4	6
(b)	6	4
(c)	7	7
(d)	4	4

10. Look at the figures given below.

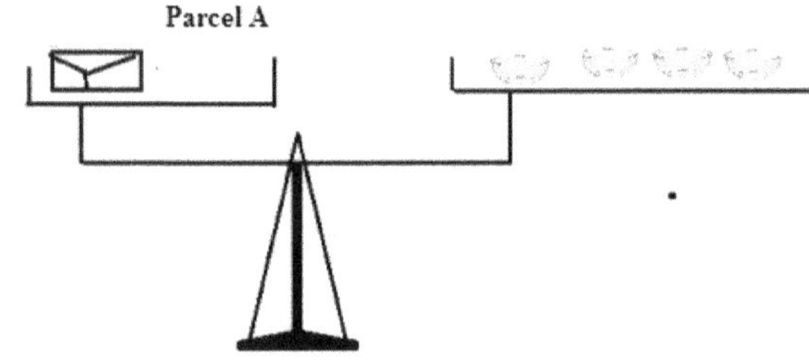

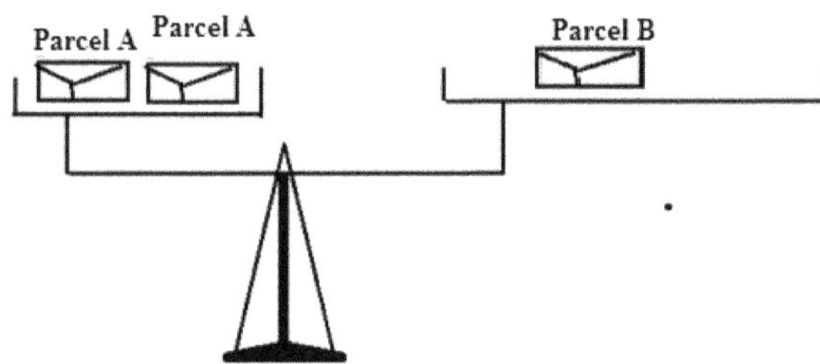

   If ⬭ weighs 100 gm, what is the weight of parcel B?
   (a) 900 gm   (b) 800 gm
   (c) 500 gm   (d) 700 gm

11. There are 70 roses in rows of 10 in a garden. How many roses are there in each column?
   (a) 17   (b) 70
   (c) 77   (d) 7

12. Sanchit wants to finish his homework within 30 minutes. He began at 3:15 p.m, but he took 10 minutes more than 30 minutes. At what time did he stop?
   (a) 3:45 p.m.
   (b) 3:35 p.m.
   (c) 3:55 p.m.
   (d) 4:15 p.m.

13. Read the given table and find the value of P, Q, R and S respectively.

Total money in hand	Purchase	Remaining Amount
(P)	Rs. 280 (Q)	P – Q = R
	Rs. 175	P – 175 = S

   (a) 300, 270, 20, 125
   (b) 300, 220, 20, 125
   (c) 300, 125, 20, 280
   (d) 300, 280, 20, 125

14. There are 200 cows in a farm. How many legs do they have in all?
   - (a) 400
   - (b) 800
   - (c) 1600
   - (d) 1200

15. If tomorrow is Monday, then yesterday was ______.
   - (a) Saturday
   - (b) Sunday
   - (c) Friday
   - (d) Wednesday

Computers

16. Who am I?
   - (a) I am a part of computer.
   - (b) I am used to store the files.

   I am also known as ____________.
   - (a) Files/drives
   - (b) Folders/dictionary
   - (c) Directory, folders
   - (d) Files/folders

17. Reena works in a Multinational Company. She is required to visit many places for her office work. Which kind of computer is most useful and helpful for her?
   - (a) Supercomputer
   - (b) Mainframe computer
   - (c) Desktop
   - (d) Laptop

18. Match column I and column II and choose the correct option.

a. ALT+F4	(i) This button is used for opening programs, documents, control panel and turning off the computer
b. Maximise button	(ii) The taskbar does not display this button
c.	(iii) We can close a program by pressing this button
d. Windows	(iv) an operating system

   - (a) a-i, b-iii, c-ii, d-iv
   - (b) a-iii, b-ii, c-i, d-iv
   - (c) a-i, b-ii, c-iii, d-iv
   - (d) a-iv, b-ii, c-iii, d-i

19. This type of wire is used to connect a computer to a mobile phone.
   - (a)
   - (b)
   - (c)
   - (d)

20. Sanchit wants to watch a movie on his computer. He switched ON the CPU. The CPU gets started but the desktop did not display anything. Which of the following could be the reason(s)?
   - i. No electricity
   - ii. UPS not working
   - iii. Display button of monitor switched OFF
   - iv. No power supply in the monitor
   - (a) i and iv
   - (b) iv only
   - (c) iii and iv only
   - (d) iii only

21. Rahul has lost a file. Which option can help him find his lost file?
   - (a) Recycle Bin
   - (b) Search
   - (c) This PC
   - (d) Network

22. Identify the object.
   - (i) Originated in China, 3000 years ago
   - (ii) Used as calculating machine
   - (a) Robot
   - (b) Abacus
   - (c) Pascal
   - (d) CPU

23. Match column I and column II and choose the correct option.

Column-I	Column-II
(i) F1 key	(a) Used to rename files and folders
(ii) F2 key	(b) Used as the help key
(iii) F5 key	(c) Used for navigation in Microsoft Office
(iv) F6 key	(d) used to "Find and Replace" words in

   - (a) i-b, ii-a, iii-d, iv-c
   - (b) i-c, ii-a, iii-d, iv-b
   - (c) i-b, ii-c, iii-d, iv-a
   - (d) i-b, ii-d, iii-a, iv-c

24. Look at the picture below. It is a set of keys of a keyboard. This set is called ______.

(a) Navigation keys
(b) Function keys
(c) Arrow keys
(d) Special keys

25. Optical mouse uses this type of technique.
(a) The Laser technique
(b) Mouse-pad technique
(c) Optomechanical technique
(d) Mechanical technique

26. Click and Drag process is:
(a) Clicking the left and right mouse buttons and dragging the mouse without releasing it
(b) Clicking the right mouse button and dragging the mouse without releasing it
(c) Clicking the left mouse button and dragging the mouse without releasing it
(d) Clicking the drag button of the mouse and dragging the mouse without releasing it

27. Ritu is drawing a picture in MS Paint. She wants to erase a part of it but due to the small size of her eraser tool, she is taking a lot of time. She wants to enhance the size of eraser tool. Which of the following key combination will help her?
(a) Alt + Numpad
(b) Shift + Numpad
(c) Ctrl + Numpad
(d) Tab + Numpad

28. Match column I and column II and choose the correct option.

Colum-I		Column-II
(a) ⬭	(i)	pentagon tool
(b) ▭	(ii)	Rounded rectangle tool
(c) ▭	(iii)	Rounded rectangle call out tool
(d) ⬠	(iv)	Oval tool

(a) a-i, b-iii, c-ii, d-iv
(b) a-iii, b-iv, c-ii, d-i
(c) a-iv, b-ii, c-iii, d-i
(d) a-iv, b-iii, c-ii, d-i

29. Who am I?

(i) I belong from the Google group.
(ii) I am a free video chat service.
(a) Wi-Fi
(b) Google hangout
(c) A social networking site
(d) An android application

30. This is not a mouse type.
(a) Fibre mouse
(b) Optical Mouse
(c) Three-button mouse
(d) Wireless Mouse

Achiever's Section

31. Match column I and column II and select the correct option:
(I) What is iPad Mini?
(II) What is iPod Nano?

	Column-I	Column-II
(a)	Smaller lighter version of the Apple iPad tablet	A small portable media player produced by Apple Inc.
(b)	Smaller lighter version of the Apple iPod	A version of the popular iTunes
(c)	Smaller lighter version of the Apple iPhone	Apples latest tablet PC
(d)	All of these	Apples latest mobile phone

32. Seema has made a picture on MS Paint. Now she wants to take a printout. Under which section she will find the Print Option?

(a)  (b) 

(c)  (d) 

33. Which of the following matches is incorrect?

Column-I	Column-II
(a) Diagnose diseases	(i) Computer in hospital
(b) Watching movies	(ii) Computer for entertainment
(c) For communication	(iii) Computers in defense
(d) Watching sports	(iv) Computers in school

34. Look at the icons below. How many are multimedia icons?

(a) 1   (b) 3
(c) 2   (d) 0

35. (I) Which OS is shown on the desktop below?

(II) How many word files are open in the computer, how will you know?

	I	II
(a)	Win 8	We will left click on the MS Word icon.
(b)	Win 7	We will left click on the MS Word icon.
(c)	Win 8	We will just place the mouse cursor on the MS word icon in the taskbar.
(d)	Win 7	We will just place the mouse cursor on the MS word icon in the taskbar.

Model Test Paper 2

1. Find the missing number.

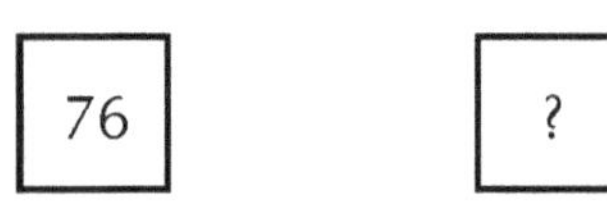

Pattern-I	Pattern-II
52	29
64	41
76	?

   (a) 40   (b) 53
   (c) 51   (d) 56

2. Who am I?
   (a) My hundred's digit is 8.
   (b) My ten's digit is 5.
   (c) My one's digit is 4 more than my ten's digit.

   (a) 859   (b) 858
   (c) 856   (d) 857

3. Swati is taller than Ananya. Ananya is taller than Aishwarya. Aishwarya is taller than Priya. Who is the shortest girl?
   (a) Swati   (b) Ananya
   (c) Aishwarya   (d) Priya

4. If yesterday was Thursday, then tomorrow will be ______.
   (a) Friday   (b) Thursday
   (c) Saturday   (d) Sunday

5. ______ is needed to buy the toy car shown below.

   (a) One 100-rupee, one 50-rupee, and two 10-rupee
   (b) Two 100-rupee, one 50-rupee, and three 10-rupee
   (c) One 100-rupee, one 50-rupee, and three 10-rupee
   (d) Two 100-rupee, two 50-rupee, and two 10-rupee

6. How many more triangles are there in the box than rectangles?

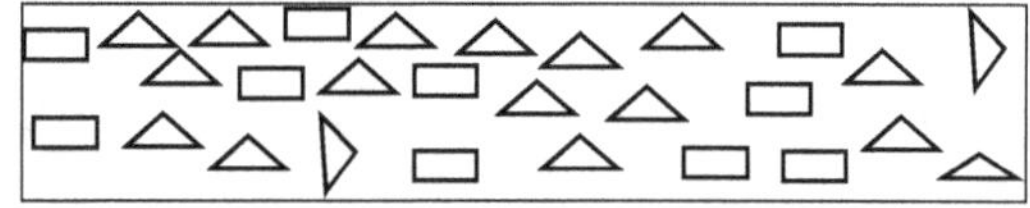

   (a) 8   (b) 10
   (c) 11   (d) 7

7. Amit resides on the second floor of the building. There are total 22 stairs to reach his house. How many stairs are there between 8th and 22nd steps?
   (a) 12   (b) 13
   (c) 16   (D 18

8. If Sumit and Shourya interchange their positions, who will be the nearest to the house?

   1. Kunal   2. Sumit   3. Shourya   4. Raj
   (a) Kunal   (b) Sumit
   (c) Shourya   (d) Raj

9. What will be the number of balls in each row, when three equal groups of 18 balls are made?

(a) 4 (b) 5
(c) 6 (d) 7

10. Which flower is the fifth to the left of the flower M?

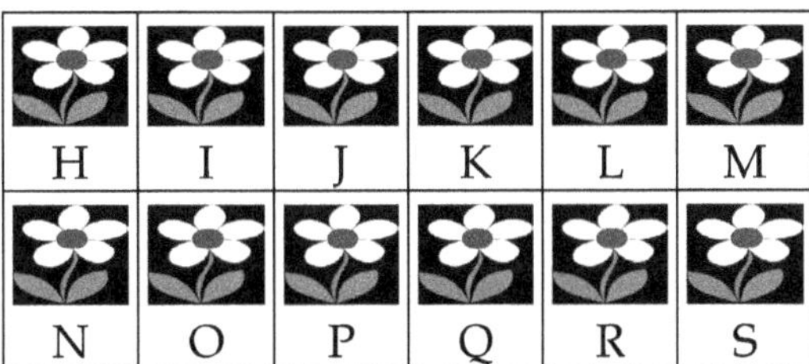

H	I	J	K	L	M
N	O	P	Q	R	S

Left   **Right**

(a) S (b) R
(c) I (d) H

11. Which of the following figures give incorrect number relation?

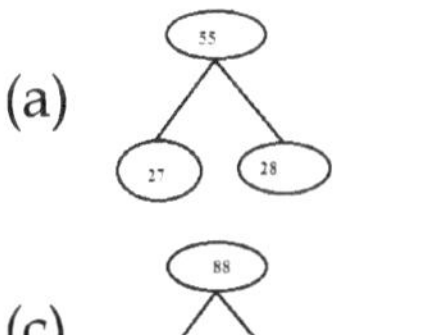
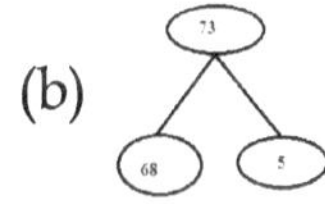
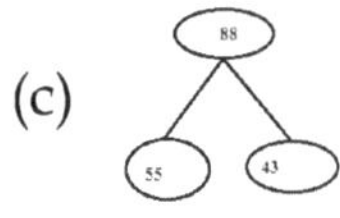

(a) 55 / 27, 28
(b) 73 / 68, 5
(c) 88 / 55, 43
(d) 42 / 20, 22

12. Which of the following item is the shortest?

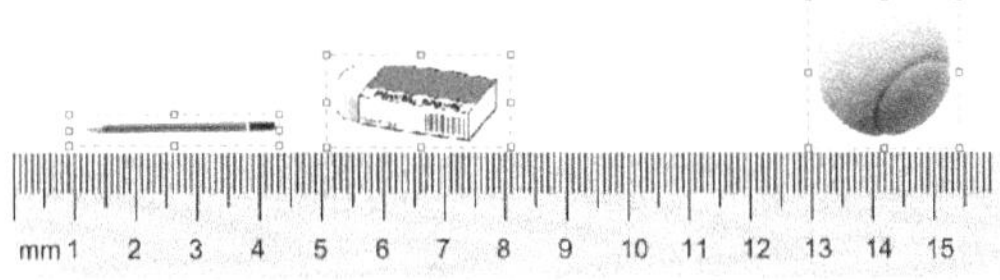

(a) Ball (b) Pencil
(c) Sharpener (d) Blade

13. Find the number of people in the queue, if I am second from the right, but fifth from the left.

(a) 6 (b) 7
(c) 8 (d) 9

14. What is to the South of the House?

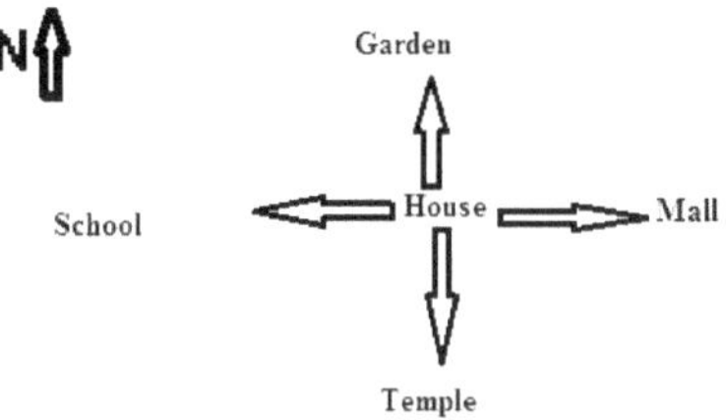

(a) Mall (b) Garden
(c) School (d) Temple

15. Swayam watched a cartoon programme which lasted 40 minutes. The programme ended at 3.30 p.m. The programme started at ______.

(a) 2.50 pm (b) 2.40 pm
(c) 3.00 pm (d) 2.55 pm

Computers

16. Match column I and column II and choose the correct option.

Column-I	Column-II
(a) Connecting wires	(i) Used for huge mathematical calculations
(b) Abacus	(ii) Connect different parts of computers
(c) Arithmetic and logic unit	(iii) Part of CPU
(d) Mainframe computers	(iv) First calculating device used by man

(a) a-ii, b-iv, c-iii, d-i
(b) a-i, b-ii, c-iii, d-iv
(c) a-iv, b-i, c-iii, d-ii
(d) a-iv, b-ii, c-iii, d-i

17. This process occurs when the computer is already ON and you restart it using the Restart option in the Start Menu.

(a) Warm boot
(b) Cool boot
(c) Freeze boot
(d) Running boot

18. These are the only two binary digits of a binary system that can be read by a computer.
    (a) 9 & 10   (b) 0 & 10
    (c) 0 & 1   (d) 1 & 2

19. Who am I?
    (i) I am an electronic device.
    (ii) I help to run the computer even during power failure.

    (a)    (b) 

    (c)    (d) 

20. This part of a computer is called the brain of the computer.
    (a) Keyboard   (b) Monitor
    (c) Disks   (d) CPU

21. Match column I and column II and choose the correct option.

    (a) Computer in office   (i) Passbook
    (b) Computer in school   (ii) Textbooks
    (c) Computer in banks   (iii) Record books
    (d) Computer in railways   (iv) Tickets

    (a) a-ii, b-iii, c-i, d-iv
    (b) a-iii, b-ii, c-iv, d-i
    (c) a-iv, b-ii, c-i, d-iii
    (d) a-iii, b-ii, c-i, d-iv

22. Look at the picture given below and answer the following question:

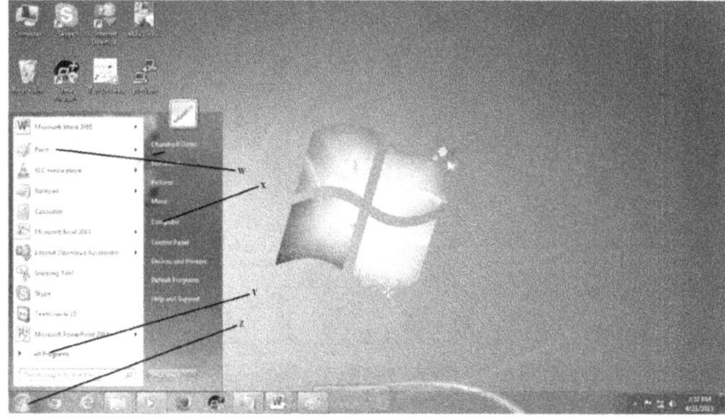

    Sonu wants to draw an image. Which button will she click with her mouse?
    (a) X   (b) W
    (c) Y   (d) Z

23. Select the correct key combination to get the @ symbol.
    (a) Shift + 1   (b) Shift + 2
    (c) Shift + 3   (d) Shift + 4

24. Look at the following pictures and match the correct key with the application.

    List-1
    (a) When we type something wrong
    (b) To write Sanchit's name
    (c) To write roll numbers of my classmates
    (d) To go back to the previous page

    List-2

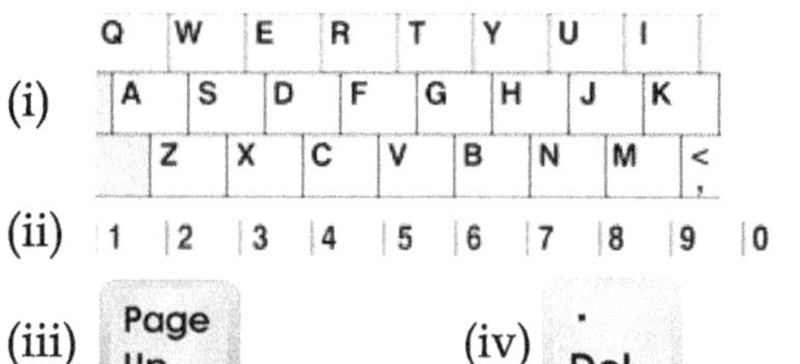

    (a) a-ii, b-iv, c-i, d-iii
    (b) a-iii, b-iv, c-I, d-ii
    (c) a-iv, b-i, c-ii, d-iii
    (d) a-i, b-iv, c-ii, d-iii

25. This term is not related to the computer mouse.
    (a) Left click
    (b) Right click
    (c) Middle click
    (d) Double click

26. Match column I and column II and select the correct option.

Column-I	Column-II
(a) Selects an item	(i) Double click
(b) Opens a window	(ii) Right click
(c) Moves an item on the monitor	(iii) Single click
(d) Shows the list of commands	(iv) Drag and Drop

    (a) a-i, b-ii, c-iii, d-iv
    (b) a-iii, b-i, c-iv, d-ii
    (c) a-iv, b-i, c-ii, d-iii
    (d) a-ii, b-i, c-iv, d-iii

Direction (27–28): Look at the picture given below and answer the questions based on the picture.

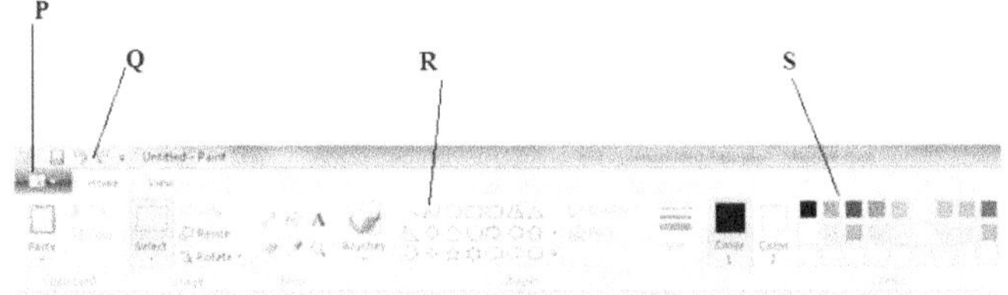

27. This area is called the Quick Access Toolbar.
    (a) P (b) Q
    (c) R (d) S

28. I help in drawing different shapes in MS Paint. I am also called the shape box. I am marked as ______ in the above figure.
    (a) P (b) Q
    (c) R (d) S

29. Mr. Bean brought a new phone recently. It has a nice big-screen. It has Android Operating System. Which of the following is the latest version of Android Operating System?
    (a) Jelly Bean
    (b) Gingerbread
    (c) Lollipop
    (d) Ice Cream

30. Small pictures present on the monitor screen are
    (a) Taskbar (b) Start button
    (c) Files (d) Icons

Achiever's section

31. Select the correct option.
    (I) What is Vita?
    (II) What is Wii?

	Column-I	Column-II
(a)	Vita is a version of a popular series of TV show	The name of a popular computer operating system
(b)	Vita is a version of a popular gaming device	Wii is a small handheld video game device produced by Nintendo.
(c)	Vita is a version of a popular TV device	A latest mobile phone
(d)	Vita is a version of a popular Computer device	A wireless internet device

32. Match Column I and Column II:

	I		II
(a)	The working speed of computer is	(i)	joystick
(b)	Computer is an	(ii)	Input device
(c)	It is used to show results.	(iii)	fast
(d)	It is used to play games.	(iv)	Electronic device

(a) a-ii, b-iii, c-iv, d-i
(b) a-iv, b-ii, c-i, d-iii
(c) a-iii, b-iv, c-ii, d-i
(d) a-ii, b-iv, c-i, d-iii

33. The data that is stored in a computer is known as
(a) Software   (b) Output
(c) Information   (d) Soft copy

34. The following information about a CPU is true.
(a) It is a miniprocessor of 1 inch square dimension and is made up of silicon.
(b) It is a microprocessor of 1 inch square dimension and is made up of silicon.
(c) It is a microprocessor of 1 inch square dimension and is made up of wires.
(d) It is a microprocessor of 2 inch square dimension and is made up of silicon.

35. Observe the image below and label the two components:

	I		II
(a)	Taskbar	(i)	System tray
(b)	System tray	(ii)	Taskbar
(c)	Icon	(iii)	System tray
(d)	Taskbar	(iv)	Clock

National Cyber Olympiad – 2

Answer Keys

Scan the QR Code to see the Hints and Solutions

Access Content Online on Dropbox: https://www.dropbox.com/scl/fi/x1il8nzpuzwm1qyz8yycu/NSO-01-Science-Olympiad-Hints-and-Solutions.pdf?rlkey=kzkx1753ie7dfs4rlkt3yo4pa&dl=0

SECTION 1: COMPUTERS AND IT

1. INTRODUCTION TO COMPUTER

Answer Key									
1. (d)	2. (a)	3. (c)	4. (d)	5. (c)	6. (c)	7. (a)	8. (c)	9. (c)	10. (d)
11. (b)	12. (c)	13. (d)	14. (d)	15. (c)	16. (d)	17. (b)	18. (d)	19. (b)	20. (c)

HOTS				
1. (b)	2. (a)	3. (b)	4. (d)	5. (d)

2. FUNDAMENTALS OF COMPUTER

Answer Key									
1. (d)	2. (b)	3. (d)	4. (d)	5. (b)	6. (b)	7. (a)	8. (a)	9. (c)	10. (a)
11. (a)	12. (b)	13. (c)	14. (b)	15. (c)	16. (b)	17. (a)	18. (b)	19. (b)	20. (d)

HOTS				
1. (a)	2. (c)	3. (d)	4. (a)	5. (a)

3. PARTS OF A COMPUTER

Answer Key									
1. (c)	2. (b)	3. (d)	4. (d)	5. (a)	6. (d)	7. (b)	8. (d)	9. (c)	10. (a)
11. (b)	12. (d)	13. (c)	14. (b)	15. (c)	16. (a)	17. (c)	18. (a)	19. (c)	20. (d)

HOTS									
1. (d)	2. (a)	3. (c)	4. (d)	5. (c)					

4. USES OF COMPUTER

Answer Key

1. (c)	2. (b)	3. (b)	4. (b)	5. (a)	6. (c)	7. (d)	8. (a)	9. (c)	10. (c)
11. (a)	12. (b)	13. (c)	14. (c)	15. (d)	16. (d)	17. (c)	18. (c)	19. (b)	20. (a)

HOTS

1. (a)	2. (d)	3. (d)	4. (b)	5. (d)					

5. LEARNING TO USE KEYBOARD

Answer Key

1. (d)	2. (b)	3. (a)	4. (d)	5. (a)	6. (d)	7. (c)	8. (b)	9. (d)	10. (c)
11. (b)	12. (a)	13. (b)	14. (b)	15. (d)	16. (a)	17. (c)	18. (d)	19. (d)	20. (a)

HOTS

1. (a)	2. (d)	3. (a)	4. (a)	5. (a)					

6. LEARNING TO USE MOUSE

Answer Key

1. (b)	2. (b)	3. (c)	4. (a)	5. (d)	6. (b)	7. (d)	8. (a)	9. (b)	10. (b)
11. (c)	12. (a)	13. (a)	14. (c)	15. (b)	16. (b)	17. (d)	18. (c)	19. (b)	20. (a)

HOTS

1. (c)	2. (b)	3. (b)	4. (a)	5. (a)					

7. INTRODUCTION TO MS PAINT

Answer Key

1. (b)	2. (a)	3. (c)	4. (a)	5. (c)	6. (a)	7. (d)	8. (b)	9. (a)	10. (b)
11. (d)	12. (b)	13. (d)	14. (b)	15. (b)	16. (c)	17. (d)	18. (c)	19. (c)	20. (d)

HOTS

1. (c)	2. (c)	3. (a)	4. (c)	5. (b)					

8. LATEST DEVELOPMENTS IN IT

Answer Key									
1. (b)	2. (c)	3. (a)	4. (d)	5. (d)	6. (c)	7. (a)	8. (c)	9. (a)	10. (b)
11. (c)	12. (b)	13. (d)	14. (b)	15. (b)	16. (d)	17. (a)	18. (d)	19. (a)	20. (d)

HOTS									
1. (b)	2. (a)	3. (d)	4. (d)	5. (a)					

SECTION 2: LOGICAL REASONING

1. PATTERN

Answer Key									
1. (a)	2. (b)	3. (b)	4. (c)	5. (c)	6. (d)	7. (b)	8. (d)	9. (b)	10. (d)
11. (b)	12. (c)	13. (b)	14. (b)	15. (c)	16. (d)	17. (b)	18. (c)	19. (b)	20. (d)

2. ODD ONE OUT

Answer Key									
1. (b)	2. (d)	3. (c)	4. (d)	5. (b)	6. (c)	7. (c)	8. (c)	9. (b)	10. (b)
11. (d)	12. (b)	13. (d)	14. (c)	15. (c)	16. (a)	17. (d)	18. (b)	19. (a)	20. (d)

3. SERIES COMPLETION

Answer Key									
1. (b)	2. (a)	3. (c)	4. (a)	5. (d)	6. (c)	7. (c)	8. (b)	9. (a)	10. (c)
11. (a)	12. (b)	13. (a)	14. (a)	15. (c)	16. (d)	17. (a)	18. (d)	19. (c)	20. (c)

4. ANALOGY

Answer Key									
1. (c)	2. (b)	3. (a)	4. (d)	5. (c)	6. (d)	7. (a)	8. (b)	9. (d)	10. (a)
11. (c)	12. (a)	13. (b)	14. (d)	15. (c)	16. (b)	17. (b)	18. (d)	19. (b)	20. (a)

5. CODING AND DECODING

Answer Key

1. (a)	2. (c)	3. (b)	4. (c)	5. (b)	6. (b)	7. (d)	8. (d)	9. (a)	10. (d)
11. (c)	12. (a)	13. (b)	14. (a)	15. (c)	16. (c)	17. (a)	18. (b)	19. (d)	20. (b)

6. RANKING TEST

Answer Key

1. (c)	2. (b)	3. (a)	4. (c)	5. (d)	6. (a)	7. (a)	8. (a)	9. (d)	10. (b)
11. (c)	12. (b)	13. (a)	14. (c)	15. (b)	16. (a)	17. (b)	18. (c)	19. (a)	20. (b)

7. EMBEDDED FIGURES

Answer Key

1. (b)	2. (d)	3. (c)	4. (b)	5. (b)	6. (b)	7. (b)	8. (d)	9. (b)	10. (d)
11. (b)	12. (a)	13. (a)	14. (c)	15. (b)	16. (c)	17. (b)	18. (a)	19. (d)	20. (c)

8. GROUPING OF FIGURES

Answer Key

1. (c)	2. (d)	3. (a)	4. (b)	5. (a)	6. (c)	7. (d)	8. (d)	9. (d)	10. (c)
11. (a)	12. (b)	13. (d)	14. (a)	15. (b)	16. (b)	17. (a)	18. (a)	19. (b)	20. (d)

9. MEASURING UNITS

Answer Key

1. (b)	2. (c)	3. (a)	4. (b)	5. (c)	6. (b)	7. (c)	8. (d)	9. (a)	10. (c)
11. (d)	12. (b)	13. (a)	14. (d)	15. (d)	16. (c)	17. (c)	18. (c)	19. (c)	20. (a)
21. (b)	22. (c)	23. (c)	24. (b)	25. (a)					

10. GEOMETRICAL SHAPES

Answer Key

1. (b)	2. (a)	3. (c)	4. (b)	5. (c)	6. (a)	7. (a)	8. (c)	9. (b)	10. (b)
11. (d)	12. (c)	13. (a)	14. (a)	15. (c)	16. (b)	17. (a)	18. (c)	19. (a)	20. (c)

MODEL TEST PAPER – 1

<table>
<tr><td colspan="10" align="center">Answer Key</td></tr>
<tr><td>1. (c)</td><td>2. (b)</td><td>3. (a)</td><td>4. (a)</td><td>5. (d)</td><td>6. (b)</td><td>7. (a)</td><td>8. (c)</td><td>9. (a)</td><td>10. (b)</td></tr>
<tr><td>11. (d)</td><td>12. (c)</td><td>13. (d)</td><td>14. (b)</td><td>15. (a)</td><td>16. (a)</td><td>17. (d)</td><td>18. (b)</td><td>19. (a)</td><td>20. (c)</td></tr>
<tr><td>21. (b)</td><td>22. (b)</td><td>23. (a)</td><td>24. (a)</td><td>25. (a)</td><td>26. (c)</td><td>27. (c)</td><td>28. (d)</td><td>29. (b)</td><td>30. (a)</td></tr>
<tr><td>31. (a)</td><td>32. (a)</td><td>33. (d)</td><td>34. (c)</td><td>35. (c)</td><td></td><td></td><td></td><td></td><td></td></tr>
</table>

MODEL TEST PAPER – 2

<table>
<tr><td colspan="10" align="center">Answer Key</td></tr>
<tr><td>1. (b)</td><td>2. (a)</td><td>3. (d)</td><td>4. (c)</td><td>5. (b)</td><td>6. (a)</td><td>7. (b)</td><td>8. (b)</td><td>9. (c)</td><td>10. (d)</td></tr>
<tr><td>11. (c)</td><td>12. (a)</td><td>13. (a)</td><td>14. (d)</td><td>15. (a)</td><td>16. (a)</td><td>17. (a)</td><td>18. (c)</td><td>19. (b)</td><td>20. (d)</td></tr>
<tr><td>21. (d)</td><td>22. (b)</td><td>23. (b)</td><td>24. (c)</td><td>25. (c)</td><td>26. (b)</td><td>27. (b)</td><td>28. (c)</td><td>29. (c)</td><td>30. (d)</td></tr>
<tr><td>31. (b)</td><td>32. (c)</td><td>33. (d)</td><td>34. (d)</td><td>35. (a)</td><td></td><td></td><td></td><td></td><td></td></tr>
</table>

Appendix

There are different organizations that conduct these examinations and covering all of them is not needed as the focus should be to understand the main type of exams conducted. They are similar for these organizations with the difference being the change in name of the exam.

Science Olympiad Foundation (SOF)		
S. No.	**Name of Exam**	**Grade**
1.	National Science Olympiad (NSO)	Class 1-10
2.	National Cyber Olympiad (NCO)	Class 1-10
3.	International Mathematics Olympiad (IMO)	Class 1-10
4.	International English Olympiad (IEO)	Class 1-10
5.	International Commerce Olympiad (ICO)	Class 1-10
6.	International General Knowledge Olympiad (IGKO)	Class 1-10
7.	International Social Studies Olympiad (ISSO)	Class 1-10

Indian Talent Olympiad (ITO)		
S. No.	**Name of Exam**	**Grade**
1.	International Science Olympiad (ISO)	Class 1-12
2.	International Math Olympiad (IMO)	Class 1-12
3.	English International Olympiad (EIO)	Class 1-12
4.	General Knowledge International Olympiad (GKIO)	Class 1-12
5.	International Computer Olympiad (ICO)	Class 1-12
6.	International Drawing Olympiad (IDO)	Class 1-12
7.	National Essay Olympiad (NESO)	Class 1-12
8.	National Social Studies Olympiad (NSSO)	Class 1-12

EduHeal Foundation		
S. No.	**Name of Exam**	**Grade**
1.	Eduheal International Cyber Olympiad (ICO)	Class 1-12
2.	Eduheal International English Olympiad (IEO)	Class 1-12
3.	National Interactive Math Olympiad (NIMO)	Class 1-12
4.	National Interactive Science Olympiad (NISO)	Class 1-12
5.	International General Knowledge Olympiad (IGO)	Class 1-12
6.	National Space Science Olympiad (NSSO)	Class 1-12

Humming Bird Education		
S. No.	Name of Exam	Grade
1.	Humming Bird Commerce Competency Olympiad (HCC)	Class 1-12
2.	Humming Bird Cyber Olympiad (HCO)	Class 1-12
3.	Humming Bird English Olympiad (HEO)	Class 1-12
4.	Humming Bird General Knowledge Olympiad (HGO)	Class 1-12
5.	Humming Bird Hindi Olympiad (HHO)	Class 1-12
6.	Humming Bird Mathematics Olympiad (HMO)	Class 1-12
7.	Humming Bird Science Olympiad (HSO)	Class 1-12
8.	Humming Bird Aptitude and Reasoning Olympiad (ARO)	Class 1-12
9.	Humming Bird Spelling Competition (Spell BEE)	Class 1-12
10.	Humming Bird Language Olympiad	Class 1-12

International Assessments for Indian Schools (IAIS) (MacMillan and EEA Collaboration)		
S. No.	Name of Exam	Grade
1.	IAIS Maths Olympiad	Class 3-12
2.	IAIS ScienceOlympiad	Class 3-12
3.	IAIS English Olympiad	Class 3-12
4.	IAIS Digital Technologies Olympiad	Class 3-12

SilverZone Foundation		
S. No.	Name of Exam	Grade
1.	International Informatics Olympiad	Class 1-12
2.	International Olympiad of Mathematics	Class 1-12
3.	International Olympiad of Science	Class 1-12

Unified Council		
S. No.	Name of Exam	Grade
1.	Unified Council Cyber Exam	Class 1-12
2.	Unified International English Olympiad.	Class 1-12
3.	Unified International Mathematics Olympiad (UIMO)	Class 1-12

Unicus		
S. No.	Name of Exam	Grade
1.	Unicus Non-Routine Mathematics Olympiad (UNRMO)	Class 1-11
2.	Unicus Mathematics Olympiad (UMO)	Class 1-11

3.	Unicus Science Olympiad (USO)	Class 1-11
4.	Unicus English Olympiad (UEO)	Class 1-11
5.	Unicus Cyber Olympiad (UCO)	Class 1-11
6.	Unicus General knowledge Olympiad (UGKO)	Class 1-11
7.	Unicus Critical Thinking Olympiad (UCTO)	Class 1-11

CREST (Online Mode)		
S. No.	**Name of Exam**	**Grade**
1.	Mathematics (CMO)	Classes KG-10
2.	Science (CSO)	Classes KG-10
3.	English (CEO)	Classes KG-10
4.	Computer (CCO)	Classes 1-10
5.	Reasoning (CRO)	Classes 1-10
6.	Spell Bee Summer (CSB)	Classes 1-8
7.	Spell Bee Winter (CSBW)	Classes 1-8
8.	Mental Maths (MMO)	Classes 1-12
9.	Green Warrior Olympiad (GWO)	Classes 1-12

How To Apply?

Anyone willing to participate in the Olympiad exam can follow these steps to apply for the exam:

☞ Log in to the official website of the conducting organization.

☞ Find the Registration Option to register

☞ Fill up the details such as Student Name, Parent Name, School Name, Class, Postal Address, E-mail Address, Password, etc.

☞ Select the subjects you want to apply for. Pay the necessary registration fees and you are done.

☞ You will receive necessary details on your email id.

There are no minimum marks required by the Olympiad conducting organizations to apply for the exam.

Awards

Based on the organization rules, students as well as schools participating in these exams are awarded with several recognitions based on the marks they score.